Building Your Personal House of Prayer

Building Your Personal House of Prayer

The Master's Plan for Daily Prayer

Larry Kreider

DESTINY IMAGE₀ PUBLISHERS, INC.

P.O. Box 310, Shippensburg, PA 17257-0310

*"Speaking to the Purposes of God for this Generation
and for the Generations to Come."*

This book and all other Destiny Image, Revival Press, Mercy Place, Fresh Bread, Destiny Image Fiction, and Treasure House books are available at Christian bookstores and distributors worldwide.

For a U.S. bookstore nearest you, call 1-800-722-6774.
For more information on foreign distributors, call 717-532-3040.
Or reach us on the Internet: www.destinyimage.com.

ISBN 10: 0-7684-2662-6
ISBN 13: 978-0-7684-2662-5

Previously Published *Your Personal House of Prayer*
by House to House Publications
ISBN: 978-1-886973-87-9

For Worldwide Distribution, Printed in the U.S.A.

1 2 3 4 5 6 7 8 9 10 11 / 12 11 10 09 08

Dedication

I dedicate this book to our Lord Jesus Christ, our teacher and model for prayer, and to my wife LaVerne and my family. To everyone who reads this book—may you find great joy in daily prayer.

Acknowledgements

A very special thanks goes to Karen Ruiz, who does an excellent job as my editor and writing assistant, and Sarah Sauder for encouraging me to write this book. Another "thank you" to those who gave valuable insight to the book: Peter Bunton, Steve Prokopchak, Ron Myer, Katrina Brechbill and proofreaders Denise Sensenig and Brenda Boll. I am also immensely grateful to Don Milam and Don Nori Jr. and all of our friends at Destiny Image Publishers. It is a joy to work with you!

Endorsements

How desperately needed this book is for me, for leaders, for all members in His Body. What I love so much about the book, is that it is profoundly simple, yet simply profound!

Jeff Farmer, President
Open Bible Churches

With the vulnerability, discernment, practicality, and powerful insight we have come to expect from Larry Kreider, *Building Your Personal House of Prayer* calls the believer in our day to remember the core, indispensable value of the practice of prayer. God is building His house of prayer, and Larry Kreider is part of the architectural team!

Robert Stearns
Eagles Wings Ministries
Buffalo, New York

This book fills a desperately needed focus on our prayer life! How can we expect to be in the center of Kingdom advancement if we are not in continual contact with the Christ who is the King? Thank you, Larry, for once again allowing the Father to use you in speaking to the present generation about the heart and soul of ministry—prayer!

Dr. Ralph Neighbour
Touch Ministries
Houston, Texas

It is wonderful to have this new book on prayer by Larry Kreider. Larry has spent much of his life establishing a true corporate body life model of congregational life: worship, cell groups, house churches, planters training and so much more. Now he has added his voice to guide the prayer life of individuals. It is a trustworthy guide. The section on "Your Kingdom Come," itself is worth the price of the book.

Daniel Juster
Tikkun Ministries International
Jerusalem, Israel

What a perfect devotional tool! Jesus had it right, as does Larry. You could have called it: "A Guide to Personal Prayer for Dummies." It is a complete guide to personal prayer!

Francis Anfuso, Senior Pastor
The Rock of Roseville
California

Larry helps us follow the blueprint given by the architect, Jesus, as we follow His master plan for daily prayer. With personal transparency, global perspective, and a heart for revival, Larry invites us to deepen our personal relationship with God in prayer. This practical guide provides prayer starters from an open Bible—the foundation of every room of prayer. Each room is graced with wisdom from those we highly regard for their life of prayer. I want to read this inspirational tool again.

Keith Yoder
Teaching The Word Ministries
Leola, Pennsylvania

12 Rooms in
Your Personal House of Prayer

Provision Room
Give us today our daily bread

Forgiveness Room
Forgive us our debts

Freedom Room
As we also have forgiven our debtors

Protection Room
And lead us not into temptation

Surrender Room
Your will be done, on earth as it is in Heaven

Warfare Room
But deliver us from the evil one

I will…give them joy in my house of prayer… for my house will be called a house of prayer for all nations.
Isaiah 56:7

Declaration Room
Your kingdom come

Kingdom Room
For Yours is the kingdom

Adoration Room
Hallowed be Your name

Family Room
Our Father in Heaven

Exaltation Room
And the glory forever. Amen.

Power Room
And the power

Contents

Ways to Use This Book 15

Introduction 17

Chapter 1   Lord, Teach Us To Pray 19

Chapter 2   Entering Into Our House of Prayer 35

Chapter 3   The Family Room 43

Chapter 4   The Adoration Room 53

Chapter 5   The Declaration Room 61

Chapter 6   The Surrender Room 69

Chapter 7   The Provision Room 77

Chapter 8   The Forgiveness Room 87

Chapter 9   The Freedom Room 99

Chapter 10   The Protection Room 109

Chapter 11   The Warfare Room 117

Chapter 12   The Kingdom Room 127

Chapter 13   The Power Room 135

Chapter 14   The Exaltation Room 141

Chapter 15   Building Your Personal House of Prayer 149

Epilogue   Revive Us Again! 161

Daily Prayer Guide 173

Using the Small Group Lessons 213

Appendix A   Who I Am in Christ 243

Appendix B   The Lord's Prayer 247

About the Author and Ministry 249

Resources from DCFI 251

Ways to Use This Book

PERSONAL STUDY

Read *Building Your Personal House of Prayer* to help turn your personal prayer life from duty to joy. Utilize the questions at the end of each chapter to apply what you've learned.

Your Daily Prayer Guide provides a valuable resource to use each day as you pray through the twelve rooms of prayer.

GROUP STUDY

Small Group Lessons provides teachers with notes to teach the chapters in the book. Questions in the outlines and at the end of chapters help group interaction.

MENTORING RELATIONSHIP

Take another person through the book as a one-on-one discipling tool.

I will…give them
joy in my house
of prayer…
for my house
will be called a
house of prayer
for all nations.
Isaiah 56:7

There is not in the world a
kind of life more sweet and
delightful than that of a continual
conversation with God.

—Brother Lawrence

Introduction

I have always believed in prayer. Or at least I thought I did. But for much of my life, prayer has been a lot of hard work.

In fact, I felt for years that there was something desperately missing in my prayer life. But that all changed, starting about six years ago. Today, daily time with God in prayer has become a great joy to me. This book contains what I learned during the past six years.

I wrote most of what you will read in this book within the past eight months, and initially published it through our ministry, House to House Publications, under the title *Your Personal House of Prayer*. The response was both overwhelming and humbling. With no major promotion, within a few months after it came off the press the entire first printing sold out. One pastor alone bought over 1,000 copies. When my friends at Destiny Image asked me to release this book with their publishing company, I updated the manuscript, added an epilogue, and renamed it *Building Your Personal House of Prayer*.

Corrie Ten Boom, the beloved author of *The Hiding Place* once said, "Is prayer your steering wheel or your spare tire?" If prayer is already your main source of direction and something you cannot do without and you are totally fulfilled and satisfied with your personal prayer life, then this book may not help you a great deal. But if you feel there must be more, read on. Expect an extreme makeover in your prayer life.

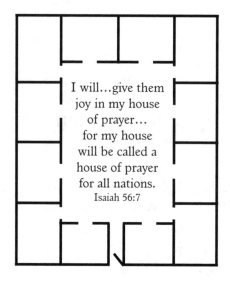

I will…give them
joy in my house
of prayer…
for my house
will be called a
house of prayer
for all nations.
Isaiah 56:7

*God rules the world and His Church
through the prayers of His people.
That God should have made the
expansion of His Kingdom to such
a large extent dependent on the
faithfulness of His people in prayer
is a stupendous mystery and
yet an absolute certainty.*

—Andrew Murray

CHAPTER 1

Lord, Teach Us To Pray

LIKE JESUS TAUGHT HIS DISCIPLES

My wife, LaVerne, and I and a small team of young leaders pioneered a new church in rural Lancaster County, Pennsylvania, in 1980 that grew into a church of more than 2,300 within ten years. It was a miracle. I had no seminary training. I had been a chicken farmer in love with Jesus, who just wanted to lead young people to Christ. In 1996, we felt we should decentralize our church into eight local churches in Pennsylvania and start a worldwide church planting movement. Today, by the grace of God, our family of churches, DOVE Christian Fellowship International, spans six continents of the world.

Despite this amazing growth, for much of my life I struggled to grow in my prayer life. Certainly, I prayed every day. I sometimes went to all-night prayer meetings. I preached about prayer, and yet I knew there was something desperately missing in my prayer life. Then I had an experience that changed my life in prayer.

Six years ago I went to Uzbekistan and met with leaders of the underground church where persecution happens in the form of fines, loss of jobs, interrogation, and imprisonment. More often than not, when I find myself in these settings, I feel that they have so much more to teach me than I can teach them, but they are typically very eager to receive biblical instruction and training.

On this particular occasion, after our team of three Christian leaders had taught from the Scriptures, they asked us questions.

One question penetrated to my core. "Tell us about your personal prayer life," one of the Uzbek Christian leaders asked. "How much time do you spend with the Lord each day?" I was suddenly uncomfortable and deeply convicted by God. I deferred the question to one of the other team members to avoid further embarrassment. I knew immediately I had been weighed in the scales and found wanting. I left Uzbekistan with a deep conviction that I must learn to pray. I fervently believed in prayer, at least I thought I did. As I said, I taught on prayer, I went to all-night prayer meetings, I prayed daily, and I knew the importance of prayer in a Christian's life. I saw countless answers to prayer in my life and in the lives of others. But prayer seemed to be such a chore for me.

I couldn't help but think that those people who raved about how they loved to pray must have a special gift from God to pray. Prayer was certainly not a joy for me. It was hard work, and although I had seasons of victory in prayer, for the most part, I wasn't as consistent at it as I knew I personally needed to be.

I scanned back through my memory of the several times I had visited Seoul, Korea, and experienced passionate prayer at Yoido Full Gospel Church, one of the largest churches in the world, where believers prayed in unison in a swell that seemed to go directly to Heaven. I remembered sitting under Pastor Cho's tutelage as he exhorted us to pray for a minimum of one hour each day. I visited this church's "Prayer Mountain" where thousands of believers spent hours in prayer, many in seclusion. I was challenged, but I came home each time finding it hard to spend an extended time in prayer.

My life was so busy; it seemed much too difficult to set aside daily time specifically for prayer. Whether I liked it or not, I was one of those Western Christians whom Pastor Cho described as vigorously taking notes on his "church growth methods," but apathetically laying their pencils down when he spoke on "prayer."

PRAYER INVOLVES ACTION

I finally came to a place where I realized I didn't really believe in prayer—or I would do it!

Suppose you were told that you had a life-threatening illness and a well-known doctor claimed to have a cure. You simply needed to submit to His guidance and prescription. If you really believed in this doctor and in his treatment, you would willingly take action immediately and do whatever he told you to do. You would act on that which you believed. You would visit him at his office to start the process immediately! On the other hand, if you didn't really believe it, you would say, "Well, let's think about it and consider it some more. Perhaps we can discern if this doctor and his cure is really as good as he claims it to be."

For some time, this is the way I responded to prayer. I believed in prayer in my head, but there was a lack of action to it. I was a busy man, traveling and writing and speaking.

On one occasion, I heard a well-known Christian leader say that he does not need to pray very much because he has a team of intercessors who pray for him. It sounded like a great plan to me! I, too, had an excellent team of intercessors praying for me daily. So I depended on my intercessors to do much of the praying for me. I more or less took the attitude, "Well, they are praying, so they can do the hard praying, and I'll preach and write and train Christian leaders!"

I finally came to the realization that if I really believed in prayer, I must take action. It's a fairly simple deduction. If we believe in prayer, we will follow up on the belief through the action of prayer. Dr. E. Stanley Jones emphasizes this common sense logic:

In prayer you align yourselves to the purpose...of God and He is able to do things through you that He couldn't do otherwise. Some things are left open, contingent upon our doing them. If we do not do them, they will never be done...except as we pray.[1]

When I visit many of the nations and cities of the world where believers are experiencing unprecedented revival, in every case, I find a people who make prayer a top priority. Two years ago, I was ministering in Manaus, Brazil, where 10,000 new believers were baptized in one day just a few months before I arrived. They were experiencing revival of this magnitude as a result of passionate prayer.

This past year, I was asked to minister at The Vine in Goinonia, Brazil, a church that grew from a handful of people to over 21,000 in eight years. They knew how to pray! It's little wonder why they are experiencing exponential growth.

I have been privileged to minister to some of the most influential leaders of the underground church in China. I noticed that leaders of these underground churches came one half hour early to each meeting to pray. No one asked them to come. They just came and stood and prayed fervently for at least thirty minutes before our meetings began. It should be no surprise that more then 25,000 people are coming to faith in Christ every day in the nation of China! The Christians have learned to pray.

I've experienced powerful prayer meetings in East Africa many times. My African brothers and sisters know how to pray! A few years ago, I was in South Africa, near Johannesburg, where people were giving their lives to Christ every week at every service. The pastor invited me to join him so I could experience the secret of the revival. An hour before the service, the pastor led the prayer meeting by walking around the auditorium as hundreds followed him, crying out to the Lord in prayer.

I ministered in Durban, South Africa, in the midst of a Muslim stronghold. One of the pastors took me to the upper room of the building, and showed me their secret. They had dedicated this room for prayer as believers met to intercede day after day for their city and their nation.

I was recently in Bulgaria in Eastern Europe. There was an immeasurable sense of God's presence in their Sunday morning service. I experienced one of their secrets—they met in small groups all over the auditorium, long before the service began, to passionately pray.

This past year I was asked to minister at a missionary conference in Waco, Texas, at Antioch Community Church. More than two thousand had gathered together to receive their marching orders from the Lord. Moreover, there was a deep sense of God's presence. And again, there was a deep dedication to prayer.

Everywhere I see God moving in a sovereign way, I see a common thread that runs through it. It is prayer! In these revivals and sovereign moves of God, God's people have learned to pray. And yet, Christians often struggle with their prayer lives more than any other area.

"LORD, TEACH US TO PRAY...."

In fact, it is an age old struggle. Two thousand years ago, Jesus' disciples seemed to have had the same problem in discovering a passion for prayer. In Luke 11:1-4, one of His disciples came to Jesus with a request, "Lord, teach us to pray..." (Luke 11:1).

There is nothing else recorded in the Gospels that the disciples requested Jesus to teach them. They never asked Him to teach them to perform miracles, heal the sick or to multiply bread and fish. But they asked Him to teach them to pray. Why?

The disciples knew Jesus prayed to His Father daily with a distinct intimacy, and they wanted it too! They had watched their Master rising up early in the morning to spend time with His Father. They saw Him going alone to pray late at night. Furthermore, they watched His life firsthand as He spoke with great wisdom, performed miracles and knew moment by moment what the Father was calling Him to do. They witnessed Jesus praying often and consistently, and they saw the results:

> *Very early in the morning, while it was still dark, Jesus got up, left the house and went off to a solitary place, where He prayed* (Mark 1:35).

One of those days Jesus went out to a mountainside to pray, and spent the night praying to God (Luke 6:12).

But Jesus often withdrew to lonely places and prayed (Luke 5:16).

Jesus went out as usual to the Mount of Olives, and His disciples followed Him (Luke 22:39).

The disciples had no doubts that the reason Jesus could speak with such authority and words of great wisdom, as the miracles literally flowed from His life, was a result of His fervent prayer life. He spent time each morning with His heavenly Father. They wanted what He had. They realized they needed help with praying. Jesus heard their hearts' cries. He knew they needed a pattern to help them grow to be consistent in their prayer lives, so He gave them a specific prayer to pray. He immediately answered His disciples, "When you pray say..."

Our Father in Heaven, hallowed be Your name, Your Kingdom come, Your will be done, on earth as it is in Heaven. Give us today our daily bread. Forgive us our debts, as we also have forgiven our debtors. And lead us not into temptation, but deliver us from the evil one (Matthew 6:9-13). For yours is the Kingdom and the power and the glory forever. Amen (Matthew 6:13 NKJV).

We call this the "Lord's Prayer" because it is unequaled for its depth and beauty. While it is a prayer that has been recited so often in a bland, autopilot monotone, if we truly understand what we are praying, it will revolutionize our lives. The purpose of the Lord's Prayer is to awaken and rekindle our faith. It is a guide to teach us to pray.

Sometimes we think we should know instinctively about praying, but if the disciples needed to request a model for praying, we do not have to feel guilty when we don't understand prayer and need help with it. As we will discover in this prayer, Jesus invites us to draw near to God and gives us twelve different types and aspects of prayer.

The Lord's Prayer is not just a prayer to say, but a way to pray. Obviously, Jesus did not intend for His disciples (or us) to repeat this prayer in parrot-like fashion. This prayer is not about rules or how to be spiritually correct. It is about a relationship and how to connect with God.

The petitions we find in this prayer are there to serve as a model. It is designed to express the *manner* in which we are to pray. On the whole, it is the most important prayer we can ever pray, and in this book we are going to use it as a model to learn how to pray.

A House of Prayer

When Jesus drove the money-changers from the temple, He said, "Is it not written: 'My house will be called a house of prayer for all nations'?" (Mark 11:17). Jesus' quotation comes from Isaiah 56:7, where the prophet declares God's house to be a house of prayer, a place set apart for sacred use. In fact, this passage in Isaiah shows us God's heart for all peoples, not just Israel.

Although the covenant was with the descendants of Abraham (see Gen. 12:1-3), it was a covenant of blessing which they were to take to all peoples of the earth. In Isaiah 56, we see God's heart for the nations, even in the design of the temple; for God provided a place where even the non-Jew could come, worship, pray, and gain access to God. The Old Testament house of prayer was to be a place of access to *all* those who sought God.

Under the New Covenant there are no special places or buildings for worship and prayer. There is free access to the Father, for all, through His Son, Jesus Christ—and that access is wherever people find themselves. We no longer need to go to a temple or even a church building to pray. "God...does not live in temples built by hands" (Acts 17:24). If we were to engage in a detailed study of the word "holy" in the Scriptures, we see that in the Old Testament it is used many times for places—but in the New Testament, it is used of God and His people; First Peter 2:9 states that we, the believers of the Lord Jesus, are a "holy" nation.

There is no literal or physical "house of prayer." The New Testament teaches, in fact, that God now resides with, and *in*, us; our bodies are the temples of the Holy Spirit (1 Cor. 3:16). Today there are many churches and ministries working together to establish prayer networks and centers in their cities and nations, and these are being called houses of prayer. I fully endorse this movement as something God is doing; but we must remember that it is never a building but the gathering of believers which constitutes the house of prayer.

For me, moreover, this image or metaphor also applies to us individually when we come to prayer. Each of us on our own, before our heavenly Father, is also a house of prayer. That is much of what we will discover together in the following pages.

JOY IN YOUR HOUSE OF PRAYER

Prayer times alone with God each day should be filled with great joy! Isaiah 56:7 describes this joy, "...I will...give them joy in my house of prayer...for my house will be called a house of prayer for all nations." I have found time alone with my heavenly Father every day to be a great joy. And believe me, after so many years of laboring in prayer (and laboring in prayer certainly has its place), I am certainly appreciating and finding joy in my daily time of prayer with my Daddy in Heaven. And so can you!

Let's be clear, this book is not about a form or a method. It is about receiving a revelation of becoming a personal house of prayer. It is about a relationship with a loving heavenly Father who desires to spend personal time with you each day. My guess is that the reason you are not spending enough time with God each day is not because you do not *want* to; you simply have not known *how* to. I have wonderful news for you! You are going to enter into a whole new world in prayer, and it will bring great joy to your life!

I believe that Jesus gave us the Lord's Prayer as a model for prayer because He wants our very lives to become "houses of prayer." The Lord's Prayer teaches us how to become a personal house of prayer. It is our manual to learn how to pray according to the example of Jesus. Since the Lord calls us to worship Him in Spirit and in truth, we need a foundation of truth in order to effectively follow His Spirit in prayer. I believe praying the Lord's Prayer is that foundation we need to get started.

Everyone can learn how to pray with some instruction. Dick Eastman in *The Hour That Changes the World* agrees,

> "Systematic prayer adds health to the devotional habit. It helps us get started and keeps us going. Most tasks in life are accomplished systematically. In fact, without a systematic approach to life, many goals would remain unreached. The same is true with prayer. The devotional exercise needs careful planning and preparation to function properly....Prayer does not come naturally to men. It must be learned....Prayer must be nourished and cultivated if it is to grow."[2]

USING THE LORD'S PRAYER AS A GUIDE

Believers from all over the world and many of the church fathers down through church history have used the Lord's Prayer as a guide to teach them to pray.

> In the very earliest Christian documents we find the praying of the Lord's prayer taught and encouraged. In the church fathers we find its meaning drawn out and taught over and over again....Throughout the ages the church has known that disciples need to be taught to pray according to the pattern and model given to it by Jesus and passed on to it by the apostles.[3]

The Lord's Prayer is sometimes referred to in ancient literature as "the Prayer." Do you remember when the disciples, along with Mary the mother of Jesus, Christ's brothers, and other believers gathered in the Upper Room after Jesus' ascension, in obedience to their Master's command to wait for the Holy Spirit? Scripture records: "These all continued with one accord in prayer and supplication" (Acts 1:14 NKJV). Brad Young, author of *The Jewish Background to the Lord's Prayer*, has concluded the Greek does not read "in prayer"; rather this verse actually states: "These all continued with one accord in 'the Prayer' and supplication."[4] In other words, the Lord's Prayer was a focus and pattern the early church used for daily prayer.

The first-century rabbis usually taught their students by giving an outline of certain topics of truth. Then the rabbis taught from each point on this outline. In His model prayer, Jesus gives an outline of various topics and instructed His disciples: "This, then, is how you should pray" (Matt. 6:9).

Pastor Cho says that he "prays the rounds" each day with the Lord's Prayer: "Like exploring the deepest ocean, it opens my eyes to new insights from the Lord and gives me a new vitality in my personal walk with God. I found that a Christian's beliefs and experiences are all contained in the Lord's Prayer."[5]

Our God is a God of patterns and plans. He gave Moses plans to build the tabernacle and later He gave Solomon plans to build the temple. Generations later He gave us the plan for salvation through His son Jesus Christ. And He has given to us a plan for prayer in the Lord's Prayer that will help our times with Him to be occasions of great joy.

Please remember that praying through the Lord's Prayer cannot be a legalistic approach to prayer. Prayer is a relationship with a holy God who loves us, not a form to follow. However, in the same way I have a healthy, growing love relationship with my wife LaVerne after 36 years of marriage, I have learned that there are certain plans and patterns God has helped me institute in our marriage over the years that have kept our marriage fresh and exciting. I plan date nights and times away with LaVerne on a regular basis because I love her; I don't do it out of legalism or obligation. This enhances our relationship. Our Master, Jesus, has given us in the Lord's Prayer a plan and a pattern to enhance our relationship with our heavenly Father that will bring great joy in our times alone with Him.

The Lord's Prayer is simply a template that I believe will help you tremendously in your personal prayer life. It has helped me, and in this book I hope to show you that, regardless if you are a mom, construction worker, doctor, pastor, or student, the most important thing you can learn to do is to pray. I am able to say that God has brought me to a place where I go to bed at night and can't wait to get up in the morning so I can pray. Praying has become such a joy to me. And after more than fifty years of prayer being hard work much of the time, this has been an amazing blessing in my life!

Praying Through Twelve Rooms

As the Lord began to give me a fresh revelation of prayer— that He has called me to become a house of prayer—He gave me a visual picture of a house. Not just any house, but a house with a courtyard in the center and rooms all around it.

In Psalm 100:4 we read, "Enter His gates with thanksgiving and His courts with praise; give thanks to Him and praise His name." To extend the metaphor a little further, I find it profoundly helpful, as I come to a time of prayer, actually to see myself entering a building, a house, with thanksgiving. I actually envisage rooms in this house, as shown in the diagram.

This style of house, typically found in Spanish and other Mediterranean places, for me is a visual aid to prayer. My understanding of the Lord's Prayer is that it has twelve key parts, and I picture twelve rooms in that house, each one corresponding to a part of the prayer. In my mind I enter this courtyard which gives me access to twelve rooms, twelve different ways to pray, based on the model of the Lord Jesus. This has revolutionized my prayer life.

12 Rooms in
Your Personal House of Prayer

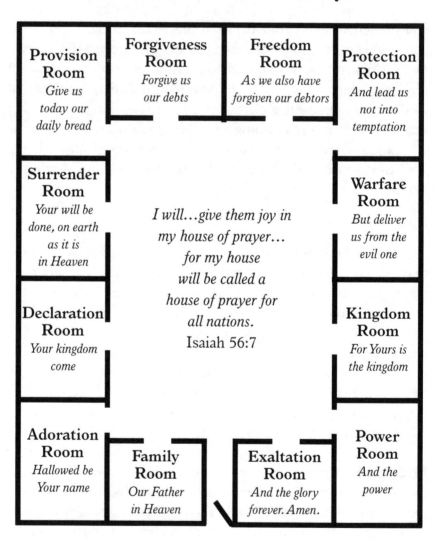

Provision Room
Give us today our daily bread

Forgiveness Room
Forgive us our debts

Freedom Room
As we also have forgiven our debtors

Protection Room
And lead us not into temptation

Surrender Room
Your will be done, on earth as it is in Heaven

Warfare Room
But deliver us from the evil one

Declaration Room
Your kingdom come

Kingdom Room
For Yours is the kingdom

I will...give them joy in my house of prayer... for my house will be called a house of prayer for all nations.
Isaiah 56:7

Adoration Room
Hallowed be Your name

Family Room
Our Father in Heaven

Exaltation Room
And the glory forever. Amen.

Power Room
And the power

What are the twelve rooms of prayer? In an abbreviated fashion they are as follows: (see Matt. 6:9-13)

1. **The Family Room**—*Our Father in Heaven,* (Matt. 6:9)
2. **The Adoration Room**—*hallowed be Your name,* (Matt. 6:9)
3. **The Declaration Room**—*Your Kingdom come,* (Matt. 6:10)
4. **The Surrender Room**—*Your will be done, on earth as it is in Heaven.* (Matt. 6:10)
5. **The Provision Room**—*Give us today our daily bread.* (Matt. 6:11)
6. **The Forgiveness Room**—*Forgive us our debts,* (Matt. 6:12)
7. **The Freedom Room**—*as we also have forgiven our debtors.* (Matt. 6:12)
8. **The Protection Room**—*And lead us not into temptation,* (Matt. 6:13)
9. **The Warfare Room**—*but deliver us from the evil one.* (Matt. 6:13)
10. **The Kingdom Room**—*For Yours is the Kingdom* (Matt. 6:13 NKJV)
11. **The Power Room**—*and the power* (Matt. 6:13 NKJV)
12. **The Exaltation Room**—*and the glory forever. Amen.* (Matt. 6:13 NKJV)

With the unique "house plan" developed in this book, you can spend several minutes in each room, and before you know it, you will become a house of prayer as you begin to develop your prayer life. Going through each room helps to build a balanced prayer life. Granted, you may occasionally want to spend daily time in only a few of the rooms instead of all twelve. Or, you may feel led to pray in a few rooms for a season of prayer and then return to your house of prayer later in the day and pray through more rooms. Let me emphasize, this prayer is not a pattern to follow legalistically, but a statement of truth to guide you as you pray, led by the Holy Spirit. The Holy Spirit is our teacher and helper, and He promises to lead us into all truth.

George Mueller, the famous Christian leader from England who established orphanages by faith, prayed with an open Bible. Take God's Word with you into each room of your house of prayer. Remember, "faith *comes* by hearing, and hearing by the word of God" (Rom. 10:17 NKJV).

Prayer was a priority with Jesus. Our Master gave us an outline with the Lord's Prayer that can take us into God's presence and satisfy our hunger to know Him and be in relationship with Him. You, too, can learn to pray and find your time in prayer to be a great joy. He will show you the best time to meet with Him each day. For me it is early in the morning. But it may be another time for you.

God wants our relationship and friendship. He will provide the time and the place. Consider Susanna Wesley, the mother of John Wesley, the founder of the Methodist Church in England.

> The mother of nineteen children, including John and Charles, Susanna Wesley still found time to pray daily. This godly saint seldom gave the Lord less than a full hour each day for prayer. "But I have no place to get away for prayer!" some might object. Susanna Wesley, likewise, had no specific place for prayer. So, at her chosen time for spiritual exercise she would take her apron and pull it over her face. Her children were instructed never to disturb their mother when she was praying in her apron. Like Susanna Wesley we must make time for prayer every day. Until we do, prayer will never become the force God intends it to be in our daily walk. Only as we apply our knowledge of prayer to the actual practice of prayer will we discover the practical power of prayer.[6]

Like Susanna Wesley, let's apply our "knowledge of prayer to the actual practice of prayer." In the next chapter, we will discover the best way to gain entrance to our personal house of prayer so we

can begin our walk with the Holy Spirit through each room. Your
life in prayer with God each day is about to change.

LORD, TEACH US TO PRAY
Apply what you've learned:

1. Are you as consistent as you want to be in spending time
   with Jesus?

2. Why do you want to learn to pray?

3. Describe a time you found joy in prayer.

4. Ask someone to hold you accountable in spending time
   with the Lord each day.

5. How has prayer at times felt legalistic to you?

*For additional prayers, and an ever increasing intimate friendship
with Jesus, see Chapter 1 in the Daily Prayer Guide.*

ENDNOTES

1. Helen Smith Shoemaker, *The Secret of Effective Prayer*
(Waco, TX: Word Books, 1976), 15.

2. Dick Eastman, *The Hour that Changes the World* (Grand
Rapids, MI: Chosen Books, 2002), 22.

3. Joel Gillespie, "The Lord's Prayer," www.covenantfellowship
greensboro.org/pages/writings/sermons/the-lords-prayer-i-overview.
php (accessed February 2007).

4. Dr. Brad H. Young, *The Jewish Background to the Lord's
Prayer* (Tulsa, OK: Gospel Research Foundation, 1999).

5. Elmer Towns, *How to Pray When You Don't Know What to
Say,* (Ventura, CA: Regal Books, 2006), 213.

6. Dick Eastman, *The Hour that Changes the World* (Grand
Rapids, MI: Chosen Books, 2002), 21.

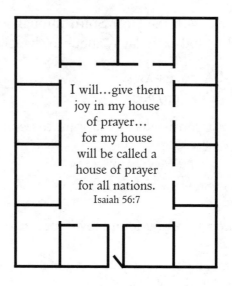

I will...give them
joy in my house
of prayer...
for my house
will be called a
house of prayer
for all nations.
Isaiah 56:7

In worship, God imparts
Himself to us.

—C.S. Lewis

CHAPTER 2

Entering Into Our House of Prayer

WITH THANKSGIVING AND PRAISE

L et's get started. Here we are at the entrance to our "courtyard home." As I imagine myself walking through the gates into the courtyard, I picture a water fountain gushing in the center of the lush gardens. Ample seating is shaded by flourishing vines and trees, lending to the tranquility and sense of safety and privacy. The comforts offered by the courtyard—air, light, privacy, security, and tranquility—set the stage for a relaxing time with a good friend. The Lord wants to meet you here. He delights in a relationship with you.

According to Psalm 100:4-5, the "password" for coming through the door and into the courtyard is "thanksgiving and praise."

Enter His gates with thanksgiving and His courts with praise; give thanks to Him and praise His name. For the Lord is good and His love endures forever; His faithfulness continues through all generations (Psalm 100:4-5).

In the Old Testament, the gates were the entrance point into the Temple complex (the dwelling place of God). As the people came through the gates, they were exhorted to come with grateful hearts for what God had done. In the New Testament, we ourselves are the temple (see 1 Pet. 2:5), so we come *spiritually* with thanksgiving and praise into His presence.

Praise and thanksgiving are inevitably linked. If we are not thankful for what the Lord has done for us, we can't praise Him for it! So *thanks* is the very basis of our praise. For example, if a friend washed my car for me, I would *thank* him and be very grateful. If he scrubbed the tires and vacuumed the interior, I would not only thank him, I would *praise* him for a job well done and even commend him to others.

We Bring the Sacrifice of Praise

To *praise* God means "to respond to God for what He has done." Praise God for specific things He has done in your life. Thank and praise Him because He is God. I must admit, I don't always feel like praising God. Praising or worshiping the Lord is not to be dependent upon our emotions, but instead on a *decision* we make.

As you come to the Lord each day, you are really offering Him a sacrifice of praise. "Through Jesus, therefore, let us continually offer to God a sacrifice of praise—the fruit of lips that confess His name" (Heb. 13:15). With your sacrifice of praise, you establish intimacy with Him. Praising and being thankful tells God that we believe He is in control of our circumstances (see Rom. 8:28). Praise is a sacrifice that we offer to God because we believe in Him and want to please Him. God is worthy of all glory and praise.

Don't be afraid to talk to yourself as you talk to God. I talk to myself all the time. The Bible says David talked to himself; he "encouraged himself in the Lord" (1 Sam. 30:6 KJV). Another time, in Psalm 103:1, we see David talking to Him, "Praise the Lord, O my soul; and all my inmost being, praise His holy name!" David was actually telling His soul to give praise to the Lord! We should be doing the same thing. I encourage you to get up in the morning and say, "I am righteous through faith in Jesus Christ. I am a man or woman of God. I can do all things through Christ who strengthens me today" (see Phil. 4:13). And then begin to give praise to the God whom you serve.

THE PASSWORD TO ENTER INTO HIS PRESENCE

To a certain degree, we are all products of our past. We learn to think in our human way about the main issues of life. The Word of God renews our minds to see life from *God's perspective* and reap the benefits that come with divine wisdom (see Josh. 1:8).

Living a life of praise and thanksgiving releases the presence of God in our lives. The Bible says that God inhabits the praises of His people (see Ps. 22:3). In other words, God "dwells" in the atmosphere of His praise. Praise actually brings us into the presence and power of God! Praise and thanksgiving is the "password" which allows us to enter the holiness of His glory. This prepares us to begin to walk from room to room in our house of prayer.

By meditating on the Word of God and praising God for His promises, we begin to see ourselves from the Lord's perspective instead of from our perspective. A new Christian will find that his soul (mind, will, and emotions) begins to catch up with what happened in his spirit when he received Jesus as his Lord. Gradually, he starts to "think like God" (he thinks according to the guidelines revealed in God's Word), instead of his past way of thinking.

God instructs us to refuse anxiety as we talk to Him and walk with Him in a constant attitude of thanksgiving. Philippians 4:6 tells us that we should "...not be anxious about anything, but in everything, by prayer and petition, with thanksgiving, present your requests to God."

When we lay our past (and present) before the Lord and begin to thank Him and praise Him for who He is and for what He has done, His peace will stand guard at the door of our hearts and minds and change us.

And the peace of God, which transcends all understanding, will guard your hearts and your minds in Christ Jesus. Finally, brothers, whatever is true, whatever is noble, whatever is right, whatever is pure, whatever is lovely, whatever is admirable—if anything is excellent or praiseworthy—think about such things (Philippians 4:7-8).

We can think on things that are good by confessing the truth to the Lord and to ourselves. Choosing to praise and thank the Lord for His goodness and grace opens the door wide for us to experience His presence in our lives each day.

WHAT PRAISE CAN DO

The power of praise and thanksgiving is so vital to our walk with God because it crowds out criticism, and helps to defeat depression and fear. Who wouldn't want these added benefits of having a thankful heart full of praise?

Just because we are praying and reading the Word does not mean we will have peace and joy in our lives. If we have a critical spirit toward others or toward the circumstances in our lives, we sabotage our peace.

The prayer of praise is our greatest weapon against a critical spirit. The Bible doesn't promise peace to those who dwell on the faults of others! It says, "You will keep in perfect peace all who trust in You, all whose thoughts are fixed on You!" (Isa. 26:3 NLT). By praising and thanking Him daily, we trust the Lord—our thoughts are turning often to Him.

Many people struggle with depression; it is an age-old problem. Even the psalmist finds himself feeling downcast, and cannot understand why. "Why am I discouraged? Why is my heart so sad?" (Ps. 42:5 NLT). As believers, like the psalmist, we know that it is not a condition we want to be in, but we find ourselves there and ponder why. The psalmist finally decides to stop asking why and instead decides to praise the Lord in spite of His depression. "I will put my hope in God! I will praise Him again—my Savior and my God" (Ps. 42:5-6 NLT). When we praise the Lord even in the bad times of depression, we are acknowledging that He is in control. By praising Him, we are allowing the Holy Spirit to minister peace to us.

Our fears—those fears deep within—can keep us from hearing from God as we enter our house of prayer. Fear of silence, fear of intimacy with God, fear of rejection, failure, and other phobias we have accumulated like fear of heights, fear of flying, fear of strangers, and many other fears can become so strong that they imprison us. The power of praise is a great weapon against fear. Filling our lives with praise by thanking Him for His love can banish fear.

Praising God tells Him that we believe He is with us and is in control of the outcome of all our circumstances. It can banish those negative emotions we struggle with because we are aligning ourselves with God's purposes when we praise Him.

Only the Lord is worthy to receive our praise. Heaven is a place that will be filled with praise and worship. Revelation 5:11-12 describes a scene of Heaven:

> *Then I looked and heard the voice of many angels...They encircled the throne and the living creatures and the elders. In a loud voice they sang: "Worthy is the Lamb, who was slain, to receive power and wealth and wisdom and strength and honor and glory and praise!"*

We don't have to wait until Heaven to praise Him. Let's begin now!

When a couple gets married, the greatest desire they have is to be in a relationship together, to spend time together. Like a plant without water, a relationship without time can wither and die. When people put their relationships first, they feel appreciated and important. They feel loved. Spending time with your spouse says, "You matter to me." Time together gives couples opportunities to renew their love, share their hopes and dreams, as well as their fears and failings.

This communication involves both speaking and listening. Our God wants us to have communion with Him and relationship with Him. Sometimes we express that relationship by being quiet and listening. Sometimes we shout to our God. Other times we talk or weep. We've been created to praise and commune with our wonderful, heavenly Daddy, and no two days in our relationship will be alike!

Are you ready to step into the first room? In the next chapter we will begin by following the model of the Lord's Prayer, "Our Father in Heaven..." as we enter the family room.

ENTERING INTO OUR HOUSE OF PRAYER
Apply what you've learned:

1. Praise God for specific things He has done in your life.

2. Tell of a time you offered praise to God when you didn't feel like it (it was a sacrifice).

3. Give an example of a time praise brought you into the presence of God.

4. Did praising God ever help you defeat criticism, depression or fear? Give an example.

5. Can you identify any current fears or an intimacy issue that would inhibit you from entering into His courts of praise and prayer? Write them down and ask God for His solutions.

For additional prayers, and an ever increasing intimate friendship with Jesus, see Chapter 2 in the Daily Prayer Guide.

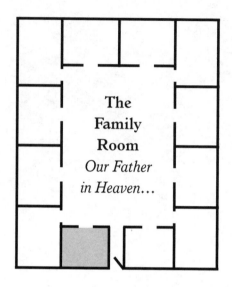

The
Family
Room
*Our Father
in Heaven...*

*True, whole prayer is
nothing but love.*

—St. Augustine

CHAPTER 3

The Family Room

OUR FATHER IN HEAVEN

When I enter the first room of prayer, the family room, I feel immediately at home. I imagine the rich aroma of coffee wafting from the open doorway; inside I notice a private seating area to hang out in—complete with comfortable soft sofas and ottomans. In another corner is a table for playing games and chatting with friends. Potted plants bloom in the windows and a bookshelf lines the far wall. A cozy fire burns in the hearth.

This is home, and my Father is here! The room's warmth and familiarity remind me that I have personal and direct access to God because He is my Father. He is my Daddy in Heaven, and He is available to me. He is never too busy to see me. I am overwhelmed by how much He loves me.

Not everyone knows this love. A friend told me that he grew up in a Christian environment but never felt His heavenly Father's love. In desperation, he prayed. For two and a half years he persistently went into the family room in prayer for the revelation that His heavenly Father loved him. He knew it in his "head" but it had to go to his "heart." Spending time soaking in his Father's love finally paid off. "It has happened!" he said recently. "I now have the assurance that I am loved by my Father in Heaven."

At a conference in Harrisburg, Pennsylvania, a well-known speaker asked the audience how many people needed to experience the revelation that they are loved by their Father in Heaven. Nearly one half of the crowd stood. I was stunned.

43

God wants to lavish His love on us. The Bible, God's love letter to us, says He lavishes His love upon us and calls us His children (see 1 John 3:1). It's like a shower of His love. There is no place in our lives that we have not experienced His touch of love, acceptance, and approval. As believers in Jesus, we are a part of a spiritual family, the family of God. And as a vital part of His family, we are loved by our Daddy in Heaven. There is no greater revelation than that! There is nothing we could ever do to get Him to love us more. He loves all of His children in His family, and He has a special place in His heart just for you! My wife LaVerne and I have four wonderful children, and they are all different from each other. But we love each child uniquely for who they are, and our God does the same with each of us!

Secure in the Father's Love

If we are to have a healthy prayer life, we must be certain of our Father's love for us and live in close relationship to Him. Only secure sons and daughters, who are totally convinced that their heavenly Father loves them, can have a vital relationship with their heavenly Father in prayer.

Why do you think Jesus' disciples turned the world upside down in a few short years? They did not change the world because they attended all the right seminars, but because they lived in close, intimate relationship with the right person! They were secure in that relationship. They were convinced that they were loved by Jesus and the heavenly Father. Let's look at the example of John, a disciple of Jesus.

The Scripture shows us that John and Jesus enjoyed an intimate, special friendship. John himself (the writer of the Gospel of John) declares repeatedly that he was the disciple "whom Jesus loved" (see John 13:23). At the Passover supper, as was customary of the Greeks and Romans at mealtime, he was in a reclining position beside Jesus, "leaning on Jesus' bosom" and he refers to himself as "the disciple whom Jesus loved." While standing near the cross during Jesus' crucifixion, John refers to himself as the "one whom Jesus loved" (see John 19:26). John called himself "the disciple whom Jesus loved" when he told Peter, "It is the Lord!" after Jesus' resurrection (see John 21:7).

John was totally convinced that he was accepted and loved by Jesus! He knew Jesus like a brother and was a devoted friend. It is clear that he was secure in the love of His Master. How did he get to this place in His life? It did not happen overnight. Jesus slowly nurtured change in John's life while bringing him the honor and recognition as being "the disciple Jesus loved."

Initially, before he matured, John's actions were less than desirable. He was hungry for status and power and seemed to have quite a few rough edges. John and his brother James were nicknamed "sons of thunder" (see Mark 3:17). I picture them as tough guys, maybe the equivalent of a modern day motorcycle gang. These brothers probably had powerful and fiery temperaments. When the Samaritans refused to allow Jesus and His disciples to come through their village, they asked Jesus if they could order fire down from Heaven to burn up this village of inhospitable Samaritans. At this point in John's life, he certainly was not modeling the Spirit of Christ!

Another time, John and his brother earned the anger of the other disciples by asking if they could sit on Jesus' right and left hand in glory (see Mark 10:37). In fact, in one case, they sent their mother to implore Jesus for special favors, showing signs of insecurity and self-seeking (see Matt. 20:20-21). Another time, John saw a man driving out demons in Jesus' name, but the man was not a part of "their group." In John's insecurity, he tried to stop Him. Jesus rebuked John for his sectarian attitude (see Mark 9:38-40; Luke 9:49).

Later, however, we see that John imparts the Holy Spirit to Philip's converts in Samaria, the very place where he impetuously wanted to call down fire on those who refused to hear the Gospel (see Acts 8:14-17; Luke 9:54). Apparently, something changed over time. As John spent more time with Jesus, his viewpoint was altered. Being exposed to Jesus' extravagant love changed John.

LOVE TRANSFORMS US

One day Jesus told His disciples the secret of His love for them: "As the Father loved Me, I also have loved you..." (John 15:9 NKJV). What an amazing promise. John received a revelation from Jesus that the Lord loved him just as much as the Father loved Jesus. In addition, the same promise applies to you and me. Imagine that! We are totally loved by God!

John also learned how to serve humbly. Jesus asked him to prepare the Passover supper, and he did it willingly (see Luke 22:8). From this, we can see the complete transformation of grace on his life. He was no longer asking for special favors, but instead was willing to serve. Like John, we need to be willing to serve the Lord in any capacity in which He asks us. When we know God loves us unconditionally, we will be willing to do whatever He says and serve wherever He wants.

The Lord taught John that love knew no bounds and should be extended even to those initially antagonistic to the Gospel— like the Samaritans. Getting to know Jesus intimately caused John to love as Jesus loved—unconditionally and fully. John wrote the first, second, and third epistles of John, and they are sometimes called the "books of love" because they are written from the heart of one who was convinced he was loved by his heavenly Father. By this time in his life, John was thoroughly secure in his Father's love. Even when John was exiled to the Isle of Patmos later in his life, where he wrote the book of Revelation, he did not complain because he knew God loved him (see Luke 22:8). Jesus molded John into a revered and loved disciple.

HE LOVES ME, THIS I KNOW!

During the early 1990s, I went through a season when I felt like a failure in ministry and leadership. Although I had served as the pastor of a rapidly growing church, I wanted to quit. With all of the outward success, I was tired, felt unappreciated and misunderstood. I felt it would be much easier to leave church leadership behind and go back into the business world.

I was encouraged to take a three-month sabbatical. It took me about five weeks to feel like a real person again. But during these three months off, I received the revelation from the Lord that my entire significance and security did not come from what I did or from what people thought of me, but instead it came from the fact that Jesus loved me, period! God loved me just because He loved me, not because of what I did.

Although I had known this to be theologically correct for years, it had never really sunk into my spirit. The song I had learned as a child: "Jesus loves me this I know, for the Bible tells me so" took on new meaning to me.[1] I was changed! Whether or not people liked me or affirmed me was no longer an issue (of course it is still nice when they do), because I knew God loved me.

I keenly remember pacing back and forth in a cabin in the mountains during this time of my sabbatical, reading aloud from the Scriptures over and over again:

> I have chosen you and have not cast you away: Fear not, for I am with you; Be not dismayed, for I am Your God. I will strengthen you, Yes, I will help you, I will uphold you with My righteous right hand...For I, the Lord Your God, will hold your right hand, Saying to you, "Fear not, I will help you" (Isaiah 41:9b-10,13 NKJV).

During this time of near burnout and disillusionment, the greatest revelation I received from the Lord was that He loved me. Period. He had not rejected me. Regardless of what others may have felt about me (real or imagined), He still loved me! I learned that my significance comes from His love for me and from His love for me alone. I was now whole because I had personally experienced the Father's love in a new way, so that I could become a spiritually and emotionally healthy servant to others. I no longer needed to perform or be good enough for God or man. I did not need the affirmation of others; I had already received affirmation from my Father in Heaven. Now, each morning alone with God, I receive anew my heavenly Father's affirmation and love.

Jesus' love relationship with His disciple John displays the unequivocal importance of developing a close friendship with God. And it all starts with us knowing that "Jesus loves me, this I know, for the Bible tells me so." It is so simple, yet so powerful! This is why it is important to enter the first room of prayer and experience the love of our Daddy in Heaven.

When Abraham Lincoln was the President of the United States, the story was told of a man who was seeking a pardon from the President for his brother. He tried to get an audience with the President, but to no avail. As he sat down to rest on the street near the President's office, a young boy walked up to him and asked him what was wrong. After hearing the man's dilemma, the young boy said, "I will take you to see the President."

"How could you do that?" asked the man.

"The President is my father," replied the boy. The boy took the man to see President Lincoln and received a pardon for his brother.

We can come boldly to the throne of grace and obtain mercy in our time of need (see Heb. 4:16). We are His children! He is a Daddy who loves us and wants us to come to Him. Our significance comes by knowing we are loved by our Daddy in Heaven.

Every morning when I walk into the family room my heavenly Father tells me how much He loves me. Without knowing we are loved by our heavenly Father, praying becomes a chore, or something we do to somehow attempt to be more accepted by God. There is nothing we can do to be more fully accepted by our heavenly Father. Regardless of what we have experienced, He wants us to come to Him to receive His acceptance and love. "...Christ accepted you, in order to bring praise to God" (Rom. 15:7).

GOD'S LOVE LETTER TO US CAN BE APPLIED IN PRAYER

Not only does God love us more than we can even imagine, our heavenly Daddy wrote a book for us, a collection of love letters. We call this collection the Bible. When I was a child, I sat on my father's lap as he read stories to me. It was a delightful, secure experience for me as a young child. And as I grew a few years older, I was able to read the stories to him. Our heavenly Father does the same for us. Imagine yourself crawling up on your heavenly Daddy's lap as He reads to you the love letters compiled in His book—the Bible. His word is filled with living power (see Heb. 4:12). Before long, we begin to read (pray) the words from the stories and letters in the book (the Bible) back to Him.

Dick Eastman, in his book *The Hour that Changes the World* says few leaders of the nineteenth century were known as much for their deep confidence in God and effectiveness in prayer as was George Mueller:

> At ninety years of age Mueller was able to declare, "I have never had an unanswered prayer." He claimed the secret to receiving answers to prayer lies in how the Christian applies God's Word during prayer. For example, George Mueller always prayed with an open Bible. He constantly filled his petitions with God's Word. Friends said the orphanage leader would not voice a petition without a "word from God" to back that petition. In fact, Mueller never started petitioning God until after he nourished himself in God's word.
>
> Describing his devotional hour, George Mueller wrote, "The first thing I did, after having asked in a few words the Lord's blessing upon His precious word, was to begin to meditate on the Word of God, searching as it were into every verse to get a blessing out of it; not for the sake of the public ministry of the word, nor for the sake of preaching on what I meditated upon, but for the sake of obtaining food for my own soul. The result I have found to be almost invariably this, that after a few minutes my soul has been led to confession, or to thanksgiving, or to intercession, or to supplication; so that, though I did not, as it were, give myself to prayer, but to meditation, yet it turned almost immediately more or less into prayer." George Mueller had learned the important secret of

transforming God's Word into faith-filled petitions. He literally "prayed" the Word of God.[2]

E.M. Bounds was a lawyer during the Civil War, who was known for his extraordinary prayer life. He spent an average of four hours in prayer every morning. He once testified:

> "The Word of God is the fulcrum (support) upon which the lever of prayer is placed, and by which things are mightily moved. God has committed Himself, His purpose, and His promise to prayer. His word becomes the basis, the inspiration of our praying, and there are circumstances under which my importunate prayer, we may obtain in addition or an enlargement of His promises."[3]

J. Oswald Sanders, in his book *Prayer Power Unlimited*, said, "The Scriptures are rich in material to feed and stimulate worship and adoration—especially the Psalms, which are God's inspired prayer books. As you read them, turn them into prayer."[4]

Andrew Murray, who developed an intense prayer life heavily saturated with the word of God once said,

> Little of the word with little prayer is death to the spiritual life. Much of the Word with little prayer gives a sickly life. Much prayer with little of the Word gives more life, but without steadfastness. A full measure of the word and prayer each day gives a healthy and powerful life.

> Our prayer time, no matter how intense, is never truly complete without the divine nourishment available only from God's Word. Indeed, the Word of God is the Christian's true prayer book. It is our guide and foundation for all effective praying. To neglect God's Word is to neglect God's power.[5]

Take some time to read from the Bible and receive encouragement, wisdom, and instruction from a Daddy who loves you perfectly. If you do not know where to start, read for a few minutes from the book of Psalms, the book of Proverbs, or from the Gospel of John. Then take a minute or so to just be silent in the family room, and receive the Lord's impressions of His love for you, both now and during any traumatic experiences of your past. When you are certain of the love of your heavenly Father in the family room, you are ready to walk into the second room of prayer—the adoration room.

THE FAMILY ROOM
Apply what you've learned:

1. Have you experienced the love of your heavenly Daddy?

2. Take a few minutes to be silent and see if the Lord gives any impressions of His love for you.

3. How have I applied God's word to my life recently? Give an example.

4. Read God's words and turn them into prayer (read from Psalms, Proverbs, or the Book of John).

For additional prayers, and an ever increasing intimate friendship with Jesus, see Chapter 3 in the Daily Prayer Guide.

ENDNOTES

1. Lyrics written by Anna B. Warner, *Jesus Loves Me,* 1860.

2. Dick Eastman, *The Hour that Changes the World* (Grand Rapids, MI: Chosen Books, 2002), 56.

3. E.M. Bounds, *The Possibilities of Prayer* (Minneapolis, MN: Bethany Fellowship, 1978).

4. J. Oswald Sanders, *Prayer Power Unlimited* (Chicago, IL: Moody Press, 1977), 9.

5. Andrew Murray, *The Prayer Life* (Chicago: Moody Press, n.d.), 107.

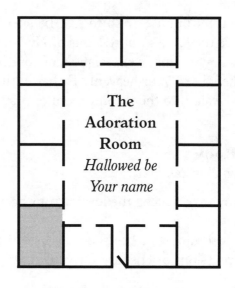

The
Adoration
Room
Hallowed be
Your name

Prayer is
exhaling the spirit of man
and inhaling the spirit of God.

—Edwin Keith

CHAPTER 4

The Adoration Room

HALLOWED BE YOUR NAME

Years ago, when LaVerne and I were choosing names for our children, a book of baby names called *What's In A Name?* was a big help. It gave long lists of names and their meanings. We poured over the names and took our time in picking one for each of our four children because we knew that this name would be carried throughout life, and we wanted to select it with much care and thought.

Names are important. Moses wanted to be able to give God a name. He wanted a name that would describe God to others. So when God told Moses to go to Pharaoh to demand that the Hebrews be set free, Moses asked God, "Suppose I go to the Israelites and say to them, 'The God of your fathers has sent me to you,' and they ask me, 'What is His name?' Then what shall I tell them?" (Exod. 3:13).

God heard Moses' question, and responded, "I am who I am." God adds, "This is what you are to say to the Israelites: 'I AM has sent me to you'" (Exod. 3:14).

The truth is, it's quite hard to nail down what God's name really means, because it isn't just something God is called, it is who He is. How do we give God a name? "I AM" carries the essence of the *God who is*. He always existed, He consists of many attributes, and He wants to reveal Himself to us in a personal, intimate presence.

GOD IS HOLY

As we enter the adoration room, we are awestruck. It is an impressive room, open and light, yet generating a feeling of intimacy and privacy. A stately room, it is not one we just barge into. We don't barge into the presence of royalty. God is holy.

What do we mean when we acknowledge that God's name is "holy"? The word *holy* means *to sanctify or set apart*. It is the expression of an intense desire that God's name be recognized, set apart, and adored. That's why we call this the adoration room. God's name is important. God is holy and to be adored and honored.

> The late A. W. Tozer, who wrote at great length about the life of the modern Church, maintained that its greatest loss today was the loss of reverence for God Himself. It was his firm conviction that God would honor any group of believers who honored Him. Whereas, wherever He was neglected or relegated to some mere religiosity, death and decadence were bound to follow.[1]

When speaking of God, holiness is one attribute that Scriptures refer to more than any other. Scripture tells us that God is "majestic in holiness" (Exod. 15:11). Isaiah 6:3 says, "Holy, holy, holy, is the Lord Almighty…." Psalm 103:1 tells us to "Praise His holy name." And we could go on and on. God's name is holy. God is holy.

To be "holy" is to be "separate." God is totally separate from anyone, anything, any imagination, and any idea. Some refer to this separateness as saying that God is completely "other." He is beyond and totally other than whatever we are or what we can think. "For My thoughts are not your thoughts, neither are your ways My ways," declares the Lord. "As the heavens are higher than the earth, so are My ways higher than your ways and My thoughts than your thoughts" (Isa. 55:8-9).

THE NAME ABOVE ALL OTHERS

The Bible says that there is a name that is above every other name. It is the highest, most powerful name in Heaven and in earth—the name of Jesus. God…

"has highly exalted Him and given Him the name which is above every name, that at the name of Jesus every knee should bow...and that every tongue should confess that Jesus Christ is Lord, to the glory of God the Father" (Philippians 2:9-11 NKJV).

The most powerful name in Heaven and in earth has been given to us "if we believe." What are we to believe?

In John 20:31 (AMP) we read what we are to believe:

...believe that Jesus is the Christ (the Anointed One), the Son of God, and that through believing and cleaving to and trusting and relying upon Him you may have life through (in) His name [through who He is].

We can have life through Jesus. Our holy God has called us to holiness and righteousness, to be holy as He is holy (1 Pet. 1:16).

There are those who will try to convince us that there are many ways to God. But we know according to Acts 4:12, "Salvation is found in no one else, for there is no other name under Heaven given to men by which we must be saved."

You Are holy as He is Holy

Because God is holy and His name is holy, we can reign in life through Jesus Christ because "those who receive God's abundant provision of grace and of the gift of righteousness reign in life through the one man, Jesus Christ" (Rom. 5:17). As you pray in the adoration room, keep your focus on Jesus and His righteousness. Refuse to be controlled by your feelings or circumstances. Rise up in faith and "reign" in life through Jesus Christ. You are righteous and have been made holy through Jesus.

The many names of God help us to understand Him. One of the most important names for God in the Old Testament is *Yahweh*, or *Jehovah*, from the verb "to be," meaning simply but profoundly, "I am who I am," and "I will be who I will be."

Some of His other names are Elohim (Creator, Mighty and Strong), *El Shaddai* (All Sufficient) and *Adonai* (Lord). Throughout the Bible, the Lord revealed Himself to mankind by many names. The Scriptures tell us: "And His name shall be called Wonderful, Counselor, The mighty God, The everlasting Father, The Prince of Peace" (Isa. 9:6).

The various names of God help us to better understand His character and divine attributes. I love to speak out in prayer the various names of God. Each name helps me recognize a different attribute of the God whom I serve. For example, I thank the Lord that He is:

The Lord our Provider, Jehovah-Jireh
This name is commemorating the provision of the ram in place of Isaac for Abraham's sacrifice (see Gen. 22:14).

The Lord our Banner, Jehovah-Nissi
This name is in honor of God's defeat of the Amalekites (see Exod. 17:15).

The Lord our Peace, Jehovah-Shalom
This is the name Gideon gave the altar which He built in Ophrah (see Judg. 6:24).

The Lord is Present, Jehovah-Shammah
This phrase expresses the truth that "the Lord is there" referring to the city which the prophet Ezekiel saw in his vision (see Ezek. 48:35).

The Lord of Hosts, Jehovah-Tsebaoth
This name was used in the days of David and the prophets, witnessing to God the Savior who is surrounded by His hosts of heavenly power (see 1 Sam. 1:3; Isa. 48:2).

The Lord God of Israel, Jehovah-Elohe Israel
This name appears in Isaiah, Jeremiah, and the Psalms. Other names similar to this are Netsah Israel, "The

Strength of Israel" (see 1 Sam. 15:29); and Abir Yisrael "The Mighty One of Israel" (see Isa. 1:24).

The Lord our Righteousness, Jehovah-Tsidkenu
This name reveals the facet of God's character that transacts the redemption by which mankind is fully restored to God (see Jer. 23:6; 33:16).

The Lord our Healer, Jehovah-Rophe
This name implies spiritual, emotional, as well as physical healing (see Exod. 15:26; Jer. 30:17, 3:22; Isa. 61:1). God heals body, soul, and spirit; all levels of man's being.

The Lord our Sanctifier, Jehovah-M'kaddesh
This name tells us God sanctifies us—"To make whole, set apart for holiness" (see Exod. 31:13; Lev. 20:7-8).

The Lord our Shepherd, Jehovah-Rohi
The primary meaning of *rohi* is "to feed or lead to pasture, as a shepherd does his flock." It can also be translated "companion" or "friend." Jesus is the Shepherd of His people (John 10:11; Heb. 13:20), and He feeds, leads, protects, and cares for His sheep. Because He is our Shepherd, we do not have to fear death (see Ps. 23:1,4,6; 1 Cor. 15:55-57).

The Lord our Maker, Jehovah-Hoseenu
This name says that it is the Lord who has made us. Since the Lord is our Maker we can put our fullest trust in Him (see Ps. 95:6). He understands everything about us.[2]

Of all of God's names, remember that He said: "I am the Lord: that is My name" (Isa. 42:8). We serve God for one reason and one reason alone. We serve God because He is God. Since the Lord has so many names in the Bible, and each one expresses an aspect of His nature or one of His attributes, when we acknowledge Him by these names, we invite Him to be those things to us:

For example, He is called Healer. When we say "Jesus, You are my Healer" and mix it with faith, it brings this attribute to bear upon our lives. This is praying a prayer of promise. One of the reasons we do not have the wholeness, fulfillment, and peace we desire is that we have not acknowledged God as the answer to our every need. We think, "He may have given me eternal life, but I don't know if He can handle my financial problems." Or we think, "I know He can lead me to a better job, but I'm not sure if He can mend this marriage." "He healed my back, but I don't know if He can take away my depression." The truth is He is everything we need, and we have to remember that always. In fact, it's good to tell yourself daily, "God is everything I need," and then say the name of the Lord that answers your specific need at that moment. Do you need hope? He is called our Hope. Say, "Jesus, You are my Hope." Are you weak? He is called our Strength. Say, "Jesus, You are my Strength." Do you need advice? He is called Counselor. Say, "Jesus, You are my counselor." Do you feel oppressed? He is called Deliverer. Are you lonely? He is called Companion and Friend. He is also called Emmanuel, which means God with us. He is not some distant, cold being with no interest in you. He is Emmanuel, the God who is with you right now to the degree you acknowledge Him in your life.[3]

Pause for a moment or two and be silent before the Lord. The God whom we serve is an awesome God! He is truly the Great I AM. Adore Him for who He is, the majestic King and Ruler of the universe. Adoration is the purest kind of prayer. It is totally for God. Tell Him you love Him! Reflect on His greatness. There is no sweeter name than the name of Jesus. The devil hates it, and men curse it, but many years ago an angel came to earth and expressed,

"And His name shall be Jesus..." (see Matt. 1:21; Luke 1:31). Whisper that name over and over in adoration.

Then get ready to enter the declaration room, declaring what He has promised—that His Kingdom will come in your life. God wants to use you to change your world through prayer.

THE ADORATION ROOM
Apply what you've learned:

1. How do you "adore" your heavenly Father?

2. Describe a time you refused to be controlled by your feelings or circumstances and instead "reigned" in life.

3. Read over the list of the names of God in this chapter and invite Him to be those things to you.

4. Spend time honoring the Lord for who He is.

For additional prayers, and an ever increasing intimate friendship with Jesus, see Chapter 4 in the Daily Prayer Guide.

ENDNOTES

1. W. Phillip Keller, *A Layman Looks at the Lord's Prayer* (Chicago, IL: Moody Press, 1976), 54.

2. These names and attributes of God are taken from *Nelson's Illustrated Bible Dictionary*, Thomas Nelson Publishers, 1986.

3. Stormie Omartian, *Seven Prayers That Will Change Your Life Forever* (Nashville, TN: J. Countryman, a division of Thomas Nelson, Inc., 2006), 108-110.

**The
Declaration
Room**
*Your kingdom
come*

*The amount of time we spend
with Jesus—meditating on His
word and His majesty, seeking
His face—establishes our
fruitfulness in the Kingdom.*

—Charles Stanley

CHAPTER 5

The Declaration Room

YOUR KINGDOM COME

As we enter the declaration room, I envision a room with a view! Sunlight pours in from the floor-to-ceiling windows which look out across the hills and valleys. A state-of-the-art sound system generates praise music to our King! We immediately proclaim, "May Your Kingdom come!" In this room we have a deep and abiding knowledge that God reigns in our hearts and transforms us more into His likeness as we declare His Kingdom to come.

WE CAN DECLARE IT!

Joshua declared, "As for me and my household, we will serve the Lord" (Josh. 24:15). Jesus declared, "I will build My Church" (Matt. 16:18). Paul declared, "I am not ashamed of the Gospel" (Rom. 1:16). John the apostle declared, "Greater is He who is in me than he who is in the world" (see 1 John 4:4). It is not presumptuous for us to declare boldly that God's Kingdom comes. We are washed clean and made presentable by the blood of Jesus. Jesus is our advocate with the Father, who sits at His right hand and intercedes for us. We are to "boldly" come to the Father with the promises He has made and ask that His word be proven true so that His glory is manifested through us.

The declaration room is the place to declare God's word over our families, our church, our communities, our circumstances, and our finances. Pray that the unsaved in your community and workplace will come to know Jesus Christ as Lord. God's King-dom and will are identical to God's Word. Read the Bible aloud in the declaration room. His word is filled with living power (see Heb. 4:12). Claim His promises as your own while staying grounded in the word.

We can boldly declare His promises because God has mighty purposes for each one of us. God is faithful to His promises. He has a specific plan for your life. Yet many of His blessings are unclaimed and ignored. In the Garden of Eden, satan said, "God is a liar and you don't need Him. You can figure it all out yourself" (see Gen. 3:4). Sometimes we fall into satan's trap, trying to figure it out by ourselves, only to end up in frustration and despair. But when we claim, by faith, one of God's promises to us, we reverse the decision made in the Garden of Eden. Every time one of God's promises is fulfilled, it shows that God's word is true and satan is the liar. For this reason, God wants us to claim His promises and not leave them lying around unused. The opportunities are end-less, "I can do all things through Christ who strengthens me" (Phil. 4:13 NKJV).

As Christians, Jesus has invited us into His Kingdom. This is so amazing to me! The God of the universe invites you and me to labor with Him in His Kingdom. It blows my mind to think that praying for the Kingdom to come is acknowledging that God is real and at work on earth right now—today! God is as active and present here and now as He is in Heaven.

> "Thy Kingdom come" is a request for God's guidance and rule in our lives. What does God do in His King-dom? He rules completely. So when we say this portion of the Lord's Prayer, we express our desire to see God's Kingdom rule on the earth as completely as His King-dom rules in Heaven. In other words, we tell God that each day we will again submit our lives to His rule on earth, just as He rules in Heaven.[1]

"May Your Kingdom come" declares that the world be transformed into a place where God reigns, where things are done by God's standards (see Matt. 6:10; Luke 11:2). Our ways are not God's ways or our thoughts God's thoughts (see Isa. 55:8). We must stand in the victory that Christ has won for us and walk in righteousness, peace, and joy. "For the Kingdom of God is not a matter of eating and drinking, but of righteousness, peace and joy in the Holy Spirit" (Rom. 14:17).

THE NEW KINGDOM IN OUR HEARTS

God sent Jesus to offer us a new Kingdom that He came to set up in our hearts. This happens when we repent of our sins and believe in the truth of His Gospel. "Jesus went into Galilee, proclaiming the good news of God. 'The time has come,' He said. 'The Kingdom of God is near. Repent and believe the good news!'" (Mark 1:14-15).

When we trust Jesus, we believe in Him and have a personal relationship with Him as Lord. We allow Him to change us from the inside out. We trust Him to change us.

An influential religious leader, Nicodemus, secretly met with Jesus in the night and told Him he was convinced that He was the Messiah. Nicodemus was a good Pharisee who believed that the Messiah would come to set up a political kingdom to free the Jews from Roman domination, and he believed Jesus would accomplish it. Jesus caught the man by surprise when He answered, "I tell you the truth, no one can see the Kingdom of God unless he is born again" (John 3:3).

Nicodemus was not ready to believe that Jesus came to change people's hearts or that they could be reborn spiritually. He could not understand that a second birth is a supernatural, spiritual rebirth of our spirit into the heavenly realm of God's Kingdom.

Indeed, understanding the rebirth requires faith on our part because it is a miracle of God. If we are born again, we start living the new life of Christ who lives in us. "I have been crucified with Christ and I no longer live, but Christ lives in me. The life I live in the body, I live by faith in the Son of God, who loved me and gave Himself for me" (Gal. 2:20).

What an amazing statement. Christ actually lives within you when you receive Him into your life! The same Jesus, who walked the face of this earth two thousand years ago, lives within you! You can stand in the victory Christ has won for you. His Kingdom is within you.

In his book, *How to Pray*, Elmer Towns encourages us to declare that God's Kingdom comes in four major areas: in yourself, in your family, in your church, and in your nation.

> **Begin with yourself.** James 5:16 says, "The effective, fervent prayer of a righteous man avails much" (NKJV). Unless you are right before God, your prayer will not be effective. Each day pray that God's Kingdom—His righteousness, joy, and peace—be established in you and that His will for you that day be set in your spirit. You need divine wisdom and revelation if you are to properly administrate your home, business, resources, and so forth.

> **Your family.** If you are married, pray for your mate. Pray that righteousness, peace, and joy will rule your mate's life. Make the declaration of faith, "Thy Kingdom come...." Pray over the needs of your mate until the Spirit releases you to move on in prayer. This is vitally important because if you lose your own house, your work for the house of God will be greatly hindered.

> **Your church.** Your third prayer priority is your church. Pray for the pastor, the leadership of the church, the faithfulness of the people, and the harvest.

> **Your nation.** Pray that the President [or leader of your nation] will have the wisdom of God...pray specifically, naming your city, state, and national leaders. Intercede for [your country]. Pray for revival.[2]

This is a great time to pray for those who do not know Christ and for missionaries in other parts of the world. I like to call this kind of prayer as having spiritual "monovision." I wear contact lenses that correct a vision error. They are called *monovision* lenses because they allow me to read my computer screen (and other up-close things) with my left eye and see into the distance with my right eye. I believe God wants us to have spiritual monovision. We pray for those who are near—in our churches and in our communities, and we also pray for those who are far—including missionaries and believers in other parts of the world.

Declaring the Word of God is so powerful. Remember, we declare God's Word to ourselves, to the Lord, and to the devil. When we resist the devil by declaring the word of God, he must flee from us (see James 4:7). Declare spiritual realities, such as, "I will never leave you nor forsake you" (see Heb. 13:5) and "I know God wants me to be restored" (see Luke 4:18) and experience the Lord's freedom in your spirit. Declare the Word of God over your life, your loved ones, your church or ministry, your business, and over your community.

Then listen to the Holy Spirit as He leads you in the declaration room to declare God's Word over persons, cities, and nations you may have never thought of. Many years ago, the Lord spoke to me in prayer that He was going to bring a man from Japan to help me in our ministry. Nearly every day for more than ten years I declared to the Lord that His promise would be fulfilled. He was faithful! God brought a man from Japanese descent into my life, who has been a phenomenal blessing to me and to the ministry that I oversee.

A few years ago, my friends, Steve and Mary Prokopchak, compiled a group of Scriptures for God's people to declare over their lives. Here are some of these Scriptures for you to declare.

I am complete in Christ. (See Colossians 2:10.)

I am an ambassador for Christ. (See 2 Corinthians 5:20.)

I am the salt of the earth. (See Matthew 5:13.)

I am the light of the world. (See Matthew 5:14.)

I am a king and a priest to God. (See Revelation 1:6.)

I am more than a conqueror. (See Romans 8:37.)

I am kept by God's power. (See First Peter 1:5.)

I overcome the world. (See First John 5:4.)

I have a guaranteed inheritance. (See Ephesians 1:14.)

I always triumph in Christ. (See Second Corinthians 2:14.)

See more promises God gives us to declare in Appendix A of this book. Begin to declare the Word as you allow faith to rise up in your spirit.

When we pray for God's Kingdom to come, we call for a drastic restructuring of our lives and priorities, because the Lord's Prayer goes on to say, "May your will be done, on earth as it is in Heaven" (see Luke 11:2). How do we move from praying these words to living them? We first have to surrender our lives completely to the Lord. In the next chapter we will enter the surrender room.

THE DECLARATION ROOM
Apply what you've learned:

1. How has God changed you from the inside out?

2. Spend time declaring God's word over your family, church, community, nations, circumstances, finances.

3. How do God's blessings go unclaimed?

4. Declare the verses in Appendix A over your life.

For additional prayers, and an ever increasing intimate friendship with Jesus, see Chapter 5 in the Daily Prayer Guide.

ENDNOTES

1. Elmer L. Towns, *How to Pray When You Don't Know What to Say* (Ventura, CA: Regal Books, 2006), 23.

2. Ibid., 85, 92, 98.

The Surrender Room

Your will be done, on earth as it is in Heaven

Prayer lays hold of God's plan and becomes the link between His will and its accomplishment on earth. Amazing things happen, and we are given the privilege of being the channels of the Holy Spirit's prayer.

—Elisabeth Elliot

CHAPTER 6

The Surrender Room

YOUR WILL BE DONE, ON EARTH AS IT IS IN HEAVEN

Let's cross the threshold into the surrender room. I
think of this room as being small and private, just
room enough for two, a place where there can be a dis-
closing of our lives with total honesty and surrender. We are safe in
the arms of Jesus here. Surrendering is trusting the details of our
lives to God.

When we pray for God's will to be done on earth as it is in
Heaven, we invite God into our lives here on earth. This opens the
door for God to change us at the deepest levels of our beings, as we
totally surrender to Him. The old hymn, "I Surrender All" says it
best:

All to Jesus, I surrender;
All to Him I freely give
I will ever love and trust Him,
In His presence daily live.
I surrender all, I surrender all
All to Thee, my blessed Savior,
I surrender all.[1]

Surrender means "to yield ownership, to relinquish control"
over what we consider ours: our property, our time, and our rights.
When we surrender to God, we are simply acknowledging that
what we "own" actually belongs to Him. We say, "Lord, my very life
belongs to You." It is a choice we must make. We must choose to

open up and share everything with the Lord as we submit to His will. God never forces us into obedience. He gives us a choice to obey and submit.

In Heaven there is already complete surrender to God. The angels are completely yielded to their Creator as they serve Him, carry out His will, and glorify Him.

I have a missionary friend who, years ago, was strung out on drugs and came from an unchurched background. As a young adult, he gave his life to God and went on to become a missionary in Asia. I asked him recently, "Why do you think your life turned around so dramatically and you never wavered?"

He didn't hesitate, "It's because I totally surrendered," he said. He relinquished control of his life and gave it to Christ. He surrendered and never turned back. Surrendering often has a negative connotation, as in "surrendering in the name of the law" or when one side surrenders to another in battle, it's a sign they've given up any hope for victory. But really, surrendering is admitting that God is ultimately in control of everything. By surrendering to God, we let go of whatever has kept us from wanting God's ways first.

When I was engaged to be married to LaVerne, I surrendered her to the Lord daily. I very much wanted to marry her, but I also wanted God's will to be done because I knew that she really belonged to the Lord, not me.

Jesus, in the Garden of Gethsemane, struggled over the longing to "Let this cup pass." But He was willing to surrender that desire: "Father...not My will, but yours be done" (Luke 22:42). At times, when we commit ourselves to prayer, our will struggles with God's will. We beg and demand and expect God to perform as a magician, because we want instant solutions. Only by submitting our will to God's can we flow into the will of our Father.

HEAVEN IS A PLACE ON EARTH!

Praying that God's Kingdom comes and His will is done to us on earth as it is in Heaven is really a plea for a transformation of our lives. Jesus said we should seek first the Kingdom of God (see Matt. 6:33). Jesus is instructing His disciples to pray that the Kingdom will come to all people—not just Jesus' disciples, but everyone should receive the benefit of living on a planet where God's will is done.

As we surrender our lives to the Lord, His Kingdom comes. As we submit ourselves to Him in every aspect, we are letting Him do in our lives and through our lives what He wants us to do. If we long to see our loved ones come to Christ, we must pray that His Kingdom comes and His will is done in their lives. One Bible translation says, "Come and set up Your Kingdom, so that everyone on earth will obey You, as You are obeyed in Heaven" (Matt. 6:10 CEV). Wouldn't it be good if everyone obeyed God? Wouldn't it be amazing if you and I obeyed God in everything?

When we pray "Your Kingdom come and Your will be done" we are inviting the Lord to bring His Kingdom power into every part of our lives as we present them to Him. We are surrendering totally all we are to Him.

Surrendering May Involve Waiting

In the surrender room we will probably spend some time waiting upon God. Scripture gives us numerous instructions for waiting on the Lord. "My soul waits in silence for God" (Ps. 62:1 NASB). "My soul waits for the Lord more than watchmen wait for the morning" (Ps. 130:6). "Those who wait on the Lord shall renew their strength" (Isa. 40:31 NKJV). Waiting on the Lord is surrendering ourselves to God.

John Bisagno observed:

Waiting upon God requires our entire being. It is not drifting into day-dreaming, but is rather an exercise that demands our keenest attention, our most alert frame of mind, and all of our soul's attention to the Heavenly Voice.[2]

The Bible says, "Trust in the Lord with all your heart and lean not on your own understanding; in all your ways acknowledge

Him, and He will make your paths straight" (Prov. 3:5-6). Notice the important word all. This is very specific. If we want divine guidance in our lives, we must acknowledge Him as the Lord over all areas in our lives. I have learned daily to submit all areas of my life to Him in the submission room. And when He shows me an area I am trying to hide from Him (which is really dim-witted on my part because I can't hide anything from God), I surrender this area to Him and find true peace.

No matter what our circumstances, if we really surrender them to the Lord, we can rest in the knowledge that God is in charge and knows what we need. He will see us through so that His will can be done.

One day Jesus said:

> "Come to Me, all you who are weary and burdened, and I will give you rest. Take My yoke upon you and learn from Me, for I am gentle and humble in heart, and you will find rest for your souls. For My yoke is easy and My burden is light" (Matthew 11:28-30).

Jesus instructs us not to allow our hearts to be troubled but to resist this by deciding to rest in quiet submission to Him and His will. We choose to say, "God, I choose this day to enter into the rest You have for me. Show me how." When we do that, God will reveal to us all that stands in our way.

SURRENDERING IS GIVING OUR CARES TO JESUS

Learning to rest is casting "all your anxiety on Him because He cares for you" (1 Pet. 5:7). For many years my father owned the field next to our home. We had large stones on our property that needed to be removed so we could have a nice lawn. My father advised me, "Just throw all of the rocks on your property into my adjacent field. I don't mind." So day after day I threw the rocks from my property onto my father's field. That's a picture of what our heavenly Father want us to do—throw our cares onto Him (He doesn't mind!), because He cares for us. Submission and resting in the Lord go hand-in-hand.

SURRENDERING IS BEING CONTENT

Submission also includes us learning to be content no matter what the circumstances are at the moment (see Phil. 4:11). When I travel to developing nations, there are times that I need to sleep in very poor conditions, and at other times I am blessed to stay at a beautiful hotel. Either way, God has taught me to be content with every circumstance. This Scripture does not say we need to delight in the circumstances but we should be able to say, "Lord, I know You are in charge. I am satisfied with Your provision and goodness and what You determine as best for me now. Therefore, I am perfectly content."

It's when we turn away from what God intends for our lives and grumble and complain that we lose our peace and contentment. When we surrender in quiet trust, we find the benefits of God's grace and rest.

Now that we have invited God into the deepest recesses of our lives and trust Him to transform us, we enter the provision room where we trust Him to supply our daily needs.

THE SURRENDER ROOM
Apply what you've learned:

1. Are you trusting the details of your life to God?

2. In what ways have you surrendered your time to God?

3. Have you ever demanded that God perform as a magician because you wanted instant solutions? Explain.

4. Describe a time you waited on the Lord for an answer to prayer.

For additional prayers, and an ever increasing intimate friendship with Jesus, see Chapter 6 in the Daily Prayer Guide.

ENDNOTES

1. Lyrics written by Judson W. Van DeVenter, *I Surrender All,* 1896.

2. John Bisagno, *The Power of Positive Praying* (Grand Rapids, MI: Zondervan, 1965), 70-72.

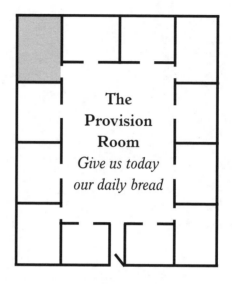

The
Provision
Room
*Give us today
our daily bread*

*It matters little what form of prayer
we adopt…or how many words we
use. What matters is the faith which
lays hold on God, knowing that He
knows our needs before we even ask
Him. That is what gives Christian
prayer its boundless confidence and
its joyous certainty. We simply make
petitions and requests to One who
has the heart of a Father.*

—Dietrich Bonhoeffer

CHAPTER 7

The Provision Room

GIVE US TODAY OUR DAILY BREAD

Our eyes pop at the colors and collection of things to see and enjoy in the provision room. I think of it as a room that is loaded with potential blessings. A full gourmet breakfast of fresh juice, fruit, home baked muffins (eight varieties), special-blend cereal, crepes, eggs, asparagus quiche, and stuffed French toast is spread on a buffet table. I expect to reap abundant blessings here! Food, shelter, clothes...everything I need is provided...just the right thing, in just the right place, at just the right time.

We may well call this room the "shopping list" room since it is here that we ask for the things that we need. God wants us to ask. He tells us that we do not have because we do not ask Him (see James 4:2). He desires to provide for us, and He wants us to ask daily.

"Give us today our daily bread" (see Matt. 6:11) reminds us that God is committed to providing our daily needs as we seek first His Kingdom. In fact, it can be said as well that when we pray first for God's Kingdom to come, we don't have to worry but can trust Him for our daily needs. It works both ways!

We can be confident that God will provide our daily bread. In the wilderness, God provided the Israelites with exactly what the people needed by providing manna for them daily (see Exod. 16:11-36). God is no less concerned for us. Just as He daily provided manna for Israel, He promises us our daily bread. We must trust in His provision and not our own.

Additionally, it is interesting to notice that the Israelites could not store up the manna for a rainy day. They could only take one day's manna at a time because yesterday's manna would be stale if they tried to store it up (see Ex. 16:19-20). The same is true of our relationship with the Lord. We have to take daily what we need from God. Yesterday's experience with God was yesterday's experience. Today we have to draw closer to God again for this day's nourishment. We can't depend on last week's experience with God. God sustains us one day at a time. That's what keeps our relationship with Him fresh and alive.

In Matthew 6:25-34, Jesus exhorted His followers not to preoccupy themselves with food and clothing, but instead He invited them into a dependence on God, like the birds and the wildflowers depend on Him. Since God provides sustenance for birds that do not have the ability to sow, reap and store, how much more can we, who have been provided with these abilities, trust our heavenly Father!

In other words, we do not have to be anxious in our asking. Rather, God instructs us to have a constant attitude of thanksgiving. Philippians 4:6 tells us that we should "...not be anxious about anything, but in everything, by prayer and petition, with thanksgiving, present [our] requests to God."

As we pray "give us today our daily bread" (see Matt. 6:11), we also must remember that we are not only asking for ourselves, but we are asking our heavenly Father for provision for our families, for those in our churches and communities, and for people in the nations who have needs much greater than we may have. God has called us not to focus only on our own needs but to become a house of prayer for all nations.

Abundant Supply

God can do "immeasurably more than all we ask or imagine" (Eph. 3:20). His supply is limitless for our lives. One of the names for God is *El Shaddai*. *El Shaddai* is the God of "more than enough." Abraham was the one who was first introduced to this revelation of the nature of God. Brian Sauder, in his book *Prosperity With a Purpose*, says that not only will we have enough (our daily bread) we will have "more than enough" (abundant blessing):

> If we examine this term closely, we find the original blessing God gave to Abraham. He was blessed to be a blessing. Abraham's God would be a God of "more than enough" to him and the generations that would follow. "Enough" is that which is required to meet our needs. "More than enough" is having extra left over to meet the needs of others.[1]

Abundant blessing is the heart and nature of God, and we find it repeated throughout the Bible. (See Exodus 36:3-7; Leviticus 26:9-10; Deuteronomy 7:13-14; 28:1-14; Second Kings 4; 2 Chronicles 20; Psalm 23; Proverbs 3:9-10; Malachi 3:10-12.) In fact, in Malachi 3:10-12, the Lord promises to pour out so much blessing that we won't have room for it. Again, we see that the God-of-more-than-enough not only supplies our daily needs but we will have surplus to give to others (see 3 John 1:2).

Many years ago, my family had a financial need. We were living on a very small budget and obeying God in every way that we knew. One day, I was praying for the Lord to provide for us financially. I opened the door of our home and I saw the most amazing phenomenon. Money was scattered on the front lawn, the porch, and all around the house—even on the back lawn! You may ask, "How did it get there?" I have no idea. Did it ever happen again? No, but I will never forget it. All I know is that God did it, and it was a blessing to us. God is a supernatural God who answers prayers in a supernatural way.

Another time, we desperately needed a larger vehicle for our family and ministry. We often picked up international leaders at the airport and needed a car that could adequately accommodate people and luggage. We started to pray for God to provide the finances to buy a larger car. God moved beyond our expectations and provided a customized van through the graciousness of a business person in our church who had two customized vans and felt the Lord told him to give us one of them. The van was so much more than what we had even asked for or imagined! God had poured out His blessing on us and provided abundantly.

LET YOUR REQUESTS BE KNOWN

Jesus gives us this advice in Luke 11:9-10, "…Ask and it will be given to you; seek and you will find; knock and the door will be opened to you. For everyone who asks receives; he who seeks finds; and to him who knocks, the door will be opened." If you lost a check with a whole week's wages, how long would you search for it? You probably would search until you found it. We need the same tenacity as we pray. We should continue to ask and thank God for His response until we experience an answer to our prayers. God may answer, "yes…no" or "wait."

It amazes me how God will answer almost any prayer that a new Christian prays. When babies are born into a family, they get constant attention every time they cry. When they begin to grow up and mature, they do not always get their own way. As we begin to grow in the Lord, we may not always get our prayers answered the same way. The Lord wants to give us what is best for us, not always what we want.

Yet, we are instructed to ask; it's that simple. "…how much more will your Father in Heaven give good gifts to those who ask Him!" (Matt. 7:11). God wants to give! I had so much fun a few years ago when I took my three daughters shopping. I encouraged them to each pick out a piece of jewelry they wanted. Of course they were abuzz with energy and excitement as they searched for just the right sparkly piece. I loved witnessing their delight and high spirits as they looked. That is how our heavenly Father feels about giving gifts to us! He is thrilled to give gifts to us. He is pleased when we ask.

Sometimes when we ask the Lord for provision He drops a creative idea into our minds for a new job or a new business opportunity. He is the Creator, and He has created us in His image. He has given us the ability to create new ideas that will provide abundant provision for both us and for others. Moses and the people of God received supernatural provision through manna in the wilderness. But God's provision for Joshua and the next generation came differently through sowing seeds and reaping a harvest. We pray, and our Father God decides how to answer our prayers for provision.

ALL WE HAVE BELONGS TO GOD

Everything we have belongs to God. We are merely managers (see 1 Cor. 4:1-2,7). The Lord gives us the responsibility to manage the resources He gives us. With this responsibility comes a reminder to give back to God. The Lord has set up a systematic way we can allow our resources to be used for God's Kingdom. It's called the *tithe* (see Gen. 14:18-20; Prov. 3:9-10; 1 Cor. 16:2).

We cannot forget it, because when we give this portion of our income to God, it shows we honor Him as the Lord of all we have. Malachi 3:8-11 says we rob God by not giving tithes and offerings; but when we do, He pours out a blessing and rebukes the "devourer."

I ministered at a church in Canada that had a unique method of giving to the Lord. Corporately each Sunday, the congregation confessed together the scriptural confession of God providing for them. They prayed for an increase in wages and investments and royalties and many other ways that the Lord provides. Faith continued to rise in the auditorium, and you could almost see the blessing God was pouring out on them. In a spiritually dry city, their church is an artesian well of life as young and old alike are giving their lives to Christ and God is prospering these precious people. They have learned to take time regularly in the provision room.

Serving God has benefits! He promises to provide. I encourage you to read Psalm 103 as you pray in the provision room. The lengthy list of benefits is vast and measureless. For example, God says:

Praise the Lord, O my soul, and forget not all His benefits—who forgives all your sins and heals all your diseases, who redeems your life from the pit and crowns you with love and compassion, who satisfies your desires with good things so that your youth is renewed like the eagle's (Psalm 103:2-6).

God also promises in Deuteronomy that blessings will overtake us if we obey Him. Here He enumerates in great detail the blessings the Israelites would receive if they obeyed Him:

If you fully obey the Lord your God and carefully follow all His commands I give you today, the Lord your God will set you high above all the nations on earth. All these blessings will come upon you and accompany you if you obey the Lord your God:

You will be blessed in the city and blessed in the country.

The fruit of your womb will be blessed, and the crops of your land and the young of your livestock—the calves of your herds and the lambs of your flocks.

Your basket and your kneading trough will be blessed.

You will be blessed when you come in and blessed when you go out.

The Lord will grant that the enemies who rise up against you will be defeated before you. They will come at you from one direction but flee from you in seven.

The Lord will send a blessing on your barns and on everything you put your hand to. The Lord your God will bless you in the land He is giving you.

The Lord will establish you as His holy people, as He promised you on oath, if you keep the commands of the Lord your God and walk in His ways. Then all the peoples on earth will see that you are called by the name of the Lord, and they will fear you. The Lord will grant you abundant prosperity—in the fruit of your womb, the young of your livestock and the crops of your ground—in the land He swore to your forefathers to give you.

The Lord will open the heavens, the storehouse of His bounty, to send rain on your land in season and to bless all the work of your hands. You will lend to many nations but will borrow from none. The Lord will make you the head, not the tail. If you pay attention to the commands of the Lord your God that I give you this day and carefully follow them, you will always be at the top, never at the bottom. Do not turn aside from any of the commands I give you today, to the right or to the left, following other gods and serving them (Deuteronomy 28:1-14).

What an amazing list of promises! These blessings are for us today as well. They are conditional upon our fully obeying the Lord and carefully keeping all His commands.

God's provision is conditional on our obedience to Him. This is why we need to enter the next room of prayer—the forgiveness room—each day, to keep our lives clean from sin, receive His forgiveness, and continue to be fully submitted to Him.

THE PROVISION ROOM
Apply what you've learned:

1. Tell of a time God provided for you.

2. Did you have to ask first?

3. Why can't we rely on yesterday's experience with God?

4. How has God answered any of the promises you asked God for in Deuteronomy 28?

For additional prayers, and an ever increasing intimate friendship with Jesus, see Chapter 7 in the Daily Prayer Guide.

ENDNOTE

1. Brian Sauder, *Prosperity With A Purpose* (Lititz, PA: House to House Publications, 2003), 29.

The Forgiveness Room

Forgive us our debts

I think that if God forgives us we must forgive ourselves. Otherwise it is almost like setting ourselves up as a higher tribunal than Him.

—C.S. Lewis

CHAPTER 8

The Forgiveness Room

FORGIVE US OUR DEBTS

The forgiveness room is a quiet, private room. I perceive it to be a room without windows, lit only by the soft glow of candles. I do not want to be distracted in any way as I allow God to search my heart.

So far, as we have been praying the Lord's Prayer, we notice how Jesus taught us to pray by acknowledging our Father and our dependence on Him and His holiness. We have asked Him to meet our needs. But now, here in the forgiveness room, the prayer directs us to consider our own sins. In fact this part of the Lord's Prayer addresses three issues: our sin; God's forgiveness for that sin; and how we access that forgiveness.

SIN—MISSING THE BULL'S EYE

Sometimes we excuse our sin because we feel it is so small and insignificant compared to other people's sin. This is very dangerous. The word "sin" in Greek is an old archery term, literally meaning *to miss the mark or the bull's-eye.* Anything other than dead center in the bull's eye is sin. So sin in our lives doesn't just mean robbing a bank, murdering someone, or living in immorality. It is so much more than that. Sin takes on many forms. We may call it a slight exaggeration, but God calls it a lie. We may call it sharing a concern about someone in the church, but God calls it gossip. We may call it looking out for our own best interests, God calls it greed.

Anything off the center of God's best and perfect will for our lives is sin. When sin is not confessed, it begins to wrap its tentacles around every part of our beings until we are emotionally and spiritually paralyzed. The agony of the weight of sin is described in the Bible by King David:

> When I kept silent, my bones grew old Through my groaning all the day long. For day and night Your hand was heavy upon me; My vitality was turned into the drought of summer. I acknowledged my sin to You, And my iniquity I have not hidden. I said, "I will confess my transgressions to the Lord," And You forgave the iniquity of my sin (Psalm 32:3-5 NKJV).

When Jesus said, "forgive us our debts" (Matt. 6:12) it has a much wider meaning than this simple prayer may imply. Here are some examples:

> Forgive us our trespasses (see Matt. 6:12 Knox).

> Forgive us our shortcomings (see Matt. 6:12 Weymouth).

> Forgive us what we owe to You (see Matt. 6:12 Phillips).

> Forgive us our resentments (see Matt. 6:12 Amplified).

> Forgive us the wrong we have done (see Matt. 6:12 NEB).

In fact, it is interesting to note that the two versions of the Lord's Prayer given to us in the Scriptures, in Matthew 6 and Luke 11, actually have different words for this verse. Matthew has the word *opheilemata*, meaning "debts" or "obligations" (see Matt. 6:12), what is legally due; whereas, Luke has the word *harmatia*, usually simply translated as "sin" (see Luke 11:2). Taken together these verses show us that it is the totality of wrongdoing, any sense of shortcoming or indebtedness which God wishes to wipe clean.

It is also interesting to note that the different vocabulary in the two versions, rather than being a point of confusion, show us that God is not concerned about the actual words we use but more with our heart attitude as we come to Him in prayer. Once again, we see that the Lord's Prayer is not a formulaic recitation of words.

FORGIVENESS

The second reflection on this part of the prayer is that God wants to major on forgiveness. The word used literally means "to untie" or "to let go." He just wipes it out and sets us free from any sense of obligation concerning that matter. It is totally dealt with in God's eyes.

When Jesus forgives our sins, He forgives them, no matter how many we have committed or how bad they were. All of our past sin is gone, wiped spotless by His blood shed on the cross. Blood, in both the Old and New Testaments, stands for death. Christ died, providing a divine substitute for us, as sinners. He became the substitute that would pay the penalty for our sin, permanently! First John 1:7 says Jesus' shed blood purifies us from sin. "But if we walk in the light, as He is in the light, we have fellowship with one another, and the blood of Jesus, His Son, purifies us from all sin."

When our dirty clothes are washed with detergent, they come out spotless. The blood of Jesus is the most potent detergent in the universe. It completely cleanses us from all sin. This purification is an ongoing work of continual cleansing in the life of every believer. As believers, we make every effort by His grace to walk in the light so that we can have intimate fellowship with God and each other.

A woman once washed Jesus' feet with her tears because she was so grateful for the forgiveness of her sins. Jesus said, "…her many sins have been forgiven—for she loved much" (Luke 7:47).

Real love for Jesus comes from a deep awareness of our past sinfulness and that He has forgiven us completely. No one can say they have made such terrible mistakes and sinned so horribly that God could never forgive them. No matter what the sin, everyone is forgiven for much, because God loves to forgive sin when we repent!

Sins Are Not Remembered

Phillip Keller, in his book, *A Layman Looks at the Lord's Prayer*, says that "forgive us our debts" could be the most important words that we ever say:

> Christ comes to us quietly and invites us to simply admit that we are wrong within and in need of forgiveness. He makes no greater demand upon us than that of sincerely pocketing our pride and seeking simple reconciliation with our Father, who is so very fond of us and so very eager to extend His forgiveness to us the moment we seek it.
>
> "Forgive us our debts" may well be the four most important words that ever cross our lips, provided we really mean them. Any man, any woman who comes to our Father in Heaven with a genuine, heartfelt attitude of contrition is bound to find forgiveness. There will fall from the shoulders the old burden of guilt, and, in its place, there will be wrapped around our hearts a radiant sense of warmth, affection, love, and acceptance. "You are forgiven. You are mine. You do belong. You are home!"[2]

When we repent of our sins, God forgives them and will never remember or mention them again. Psalm 103:12 tells us that "as far as the east is from the west, so far has He removed our transgressions from us."

You can't get any farther than that! It is as far as you can imagine. When Jesus forgives our sins, He forgets them, period. God gives us a wonderful promise in Micah 7:19. He says He will "...tread our sins underfoot and hurl all our iniquities into the depths of the sea."

This promise paints an awesome word picture. Our sins sink to the depths of the ocean, never to rise again. God not only casts our sins into the deepest sea, I believe He puts a sign there that says, "No Fishing!"

When the Egyptians pursued the Israelites through the Red Sea, there was not one Egyptian left to pursue God's people. They all perished in the sea. Likewise, no sin we have confessed can survive God's forgiveness. Like the Egyptians and their chariots, our sins "...sank like lead in the mighty waters" (Exod. 15:10). Our sins are totally forgiven, never to be remembered again. The Lord has forgotten our sins as if they have never been, and He wants us to forget them too. We are totally set free when Jesus forgives our sins. Each day we can be restored to God's fellowship when we ask for forgiveness.

CONFESSION

As we mentioned earlier, this part of the Lord's Prayer mentions our sin; it tells us of God's forgiveness. Additionally, it teaches us how to move from sin to forgiveness—that is, how to access the amazing forgiveness of God. And it is simple—we ask for it! "Forgive us our debts" (Matt. 6:12)! In the local church, we usually call this aspect of prayer "confession."

What is confession? The New Testament Greek word for *confess* means "to agree with God" concerning His opinion of a matter. It also means "to admit my guilt." It acknowledges that we really do need God's forgiveness. When we confess our sins we are agreeing with God concerning the sin in our lives, as revealed through His Word by the Holy Spirit. Confession is to verbalize our spiritual shortcomings and admit we have sinned.

Simply stated, confession is the act of declared admission. At no other time in prayer does the believer look so carefully at his own spiritual growth as during confession. Both King David and Solomon spoke of this as communing with their own hearts. Dwight L. Moody called it a "personal debate betwixt ourselves and our hearts." Defining this aspect of prayer, Moody added, "Commune—or hold a serious communication and clear intelligence and acquaintance—with your own hearts."[3]

If any sins in our lives remain unconfessed, we will be weighed down, and eventually the sins will paralyze us. To make matters worse, the Scriptures teach us that if we have sin in our lives, the Lord may not be listening to our prayers. King David said, "If I had cherished sin in my heart, the Lord would not have listened; but God has surely listened and heard my voice in prayer. Praise be to God, who has not rejected my prayer or withheld His love from me!" (Ps. 66:18-20).

Stormie Omartian, in her book *Seven Prayers That Will Change Your Life Forever*, says, "When sin is left unconfessed, a wall goes up between you and God. Even though the sin may have stopped, if it hasn't been confessed before the Lord, it will still weigh you down, dragging you back toward the past you are trying to leave behind. I know because I used to carry around a bag of failures on my back that was so heavy I could barely move. I didn't realize how spiritually stooped over I had become. When I finally confessed my sins, I actually felt the weight being lifted."[4]

> The devil has a hook in you wherever there is unconfessed sin. Repeated returns to the same sin are no excuse for not confessing. You must keep your life totally open before the Lord if you want to be delivered from the bondage of sin. You can't be delivered from something you have not put out of your life. Confessing is speaking the whole truth about your sin. Renouncing is taking a firm stand against it and removing its right to stay. Because we are not perfect, confession and repentance are ongoing. There are always new levels of Jesus' life that need to be worked in us. We fall short of the glory of God in ways that we can't yet even imagine.[5]

THE PRAYER OF CONFESSION HEALS YOUR HEART

In the forgiveness room, we daily endeavor to keep our hearts pure. Someone once said that "every major spiritual failure begins as a tiny seed of misconduct." During your times of confession be on guard for little things—those unseen sins that grow to cause such severe damage. Virginia Whitman, in her book *The Excitement of Answered Prayer,* tells of an incident that occurred in New York City. "Someone tossed an empty beverage can in front of a subway train just as it was entering a tunnel. It was only a tin can but somehow that can landed on the 'live' electrical rail, causing a major power failure. The result was an hour and a half delay that affected an amazing 55 trains and 75,000 passengers."[6] A hidden or unnoticed sin has the potential to cause disorder and destruction in our lives.

Every day in the forgiveness room, we should do a spiritual house cleaning. This is the kind of housekeeping that goes beyond what others see and hear. It's not just a light dusting, but a cleansing from within—inside and out. We must ask the Lord to cleanse those sins that we are not even aware of so they can be rooted out and confessed and forgiven. We open our hearts and allow ourselves to get spiritually healthy.

Harold Lindsell writes, "Just as the surgeon lances a boil to permit the infection to drain and to heal from the inside, so confession opens the sore, drains the poison, and heals from within."[7] There can be no healing *inside* until there is first confession *outside.* Confession is a condition of cleansing. The Bible encourages us to confess our sin and reach out for help. When our spiritual closets are clean, the heaviness from hidden sin will lift and we are healed.

The good news is that we can come daily before the Lord and lay our sins at the foot of the cross. Confessing is an ongoing activity because we are not perfect. God wants us to be real with both ourselves and with Him. If we "fall short of the glory of God" (Rom. 3:23) we should request His forgiveness. The Bible says:

> *If we claim to be without sin, we deceive ourselves and the truth is not in us. If we confess our sins, He is faithful and just and will forgive us our sins and purify us from all unrighteousness. If we claim we have not sinned, we make Him out to be a liar and His word has no place in our lives. My dear children, I write this to you so that you will not sin. But if anybody does sin, we have one who speaks to the Father in our*

*defense—Jesus Christ, the Righteous One. He is the atoning
sacrifice for our sins, and not only for ours but also for the sins
of the whole world* (1 John 1:8-10; 2:1-2).

THE DEVIL CONDEMNS; GOD CONVICTS

Sometimes people struggle with "false guilt." It is something
that feels like guilt, but it is really just shame. It is the leftover negative feelings from our sinful past. False guilt causes us to hang on
to our feelings of being dirty and sinful, even after we have confessed our sins and God has forgiven us.

The enemy uses false guilt to plague many of God's people.
Before I received Jesus as my Lord, I experienced genuine guilt
over my sins. Yet even after I received the Lord, the guilt continued
although I was totally forgiven from God's perspective. Then I
read God's word, "If we confess our sins, He is faithful and just
and will forgive us our sins and purify us from all unrighteous-
ness" (1 John 1:9). I took this promise literally and confessed it
aloud, over and over again, until faith rose up in my spirit and I
really believed it.

From that moment on, I stopped living by past experiences,
feelings, and fears. I started living by the word of God, and the
guilt left. I knew I was forgiven because the Bible told me so! I
remembered that God had removed my sins "as far as the east is
from the west" (Ps. 103:12). I was safe from all condemnation for
my sins. It was as if they had not been committed at all. That is
how freely God forgives when we place our trust in Him!

The devil will tell us that it is a long way back to God when
we sin. He will try to make us believe that God will never use us
again. But we now know better. If we sin, we must confess our sins
and repent (we stop it and we change our direction). The Lord forgives us, and we start with a new, clean slate.

Sometimes restitution has to follow repentance. This is put-
ting things right with people we have wronged. If someone
repents from shoplifting, he needs to pay it back. Although he is
forgiven the moment he confesses his sin, he needs to take a step of

obedience and restore what was stolen. When Zacchaeus repented for running a crooked tax collection agency, he told the Lord he would restore four times what he stole (see Luke 19:8-9).

Let's pray along with David, "See if there is any wicked way in me, and lead me in the way everlasting" (Ps. 139:24 NKJV). "Create in me a pure heart, O God, and renew a steadfast spirit within me" (Ps. 51:10).

Take some time to be still before the Lord to see if He reveals anything you may have missed. He will be faithful to show you because He has made the way for you to live in freedom through Christ. And speaking of freedom, let's walk into our next room of prayer—the freedom room.

THE FORGIVENESS ROOM
Apply what you've learned:

1. Has unconfessed sin ever weighed you down? How?

2. Share a personal forgiveness story with someone.

3. How has healing occurred as a result of confessing sin in your life?

4. Have you ever experienced false guilt? Why?

For additional prayers, and an ever increasing intimate friendship with Jesus, see Chapter 8 in the Daily Prayer Guide.

ENDNOTES

1. W. Phillip Keller, *A Layman Looks at the Lord's Prayer* (Chicago: IL Moody Press, 1976), 111.

2. Ibid., 116.

3. Dick Eastman, *The Hour That Changes the World* (Grand Rapids, MI: Chosen Books, 2002), 45.

4. Stormie Omartian, *Seven Prayers That Will Change Your Life Forever* (Nashville, TN: J. Countryman, a division of Thomas Nelson, Inc., 2006), 17-18.

5. Ibid., 22.

6. Virginia Whitman, *The Excitement of Answered Prayer* (Waco, TX: Word Books, 1967), 64.

7. Harold Lindsell, *When You Pray* (Grand Rapids, MI: Baker Book House, 1975).

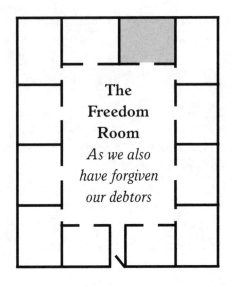

The Freedom Room

As we also have forgiven our debtors

*If we really want to love
we must learn how to forgive.*

—Mother Teresa

CHAPTER 9

The Freedom Room

AS WE ALSO HAVE FORGIVEN OUR DEBTORS

The freedom room is spacious and inviting with lots of light pouring in from the skylight in the ceiling. It's an expansive room that allows freedom of movement—it reminds us of the freedom the Lord wants us to have in all areas of our lives.

To obtain this freedom, we hold an important scriptural key in this room. Matthew 6:14-15, says, "For if you forgive men when they sin against you, your heavenly Father will also forgive you. But if you do not forgive men their sins, your Father will not forgive your sins" (Matt. 6:14-15).

This is important! *We must forgive those who have sinned against us in order for God to forgive us.* This is the room where we pray for freedom to come into our lives. It is where we should search our hearts to see if there is anything there that even resembles unforgiveness.

In Matthew 18, Jesus tells a parable about a servant who owed his king a large amount of money (let's say one million dollars). He begged the king for extra time to pay the debt, and the king had pity on him and canceled the whole debt. The servant then went out and found one of his fellow servants who owed him a much smaller amount (let's say two thousand dollars). He grabbed him by the shirt and demanded immediate payment. The fellow servant pleaded for more time, but the servant refused and had him thrown into prison. (See Matthew 18:23-30.)

The king discovered what had happened and called the servant in. "I forgave you a million dollars and you couldn't forgive someone a few thousand dollars? I showed you mercy but you could not show mercy to another?" (see Matt. 18:31-33). Then the Scripture makes an interesting statement, "In anger his master turned him over to the jailers to be tortured, until he should pay back all he owed. This is how my heavenly Father will treat each of you unless you forgive your brother from your heart" (Matt. 18:34-35).

The king had the man thrown into prison for not showing forgiveness to another. Jesus says that if we don't forgive someone who has hurt us or "ripped us off," God will deliver us to the *torturers* or *demons of hell*. Even Christians, if they choose not to forgive, can be tormented with confusion, frustration, depression, and other ailments brought on by the demons of hell. Unforgiveness leaves the door wide open for the devil!

We have been forgiven for so much. Dr. Martyn Lloyd Jones, the great minister of London, wrote, "Whenever I see myself before God and realize something of what my blessed Lord has done for me at Calvary, I am ready to forgive anybody anything. I cannot withhold it. I do not even want to withhold it."[1]

KEEP SHORT ACCOUNTS

Why do we need to forgive every day? Hebrews 12:15 says it like this: "See to it that no one misses the grace of God and that no bitter root grows up to cause trouble and defile many." Bitterness starts out like a small root. Did you ever see a sidewalk where roots had pushed up and cracked the concrete? It started with just one little root. We must keep short accounts.

To keep short accounts means to not let small issues build up into larger ones. We must forgive others quickly and fully. Try walking around with a cement block tied to your belt. A person you have not forgiven controls your life because you carry that individual with you. Forgiving does not mean that what that individual did or said was right! It was wrong, but forgiving sets you free.

During WWII in France, a young nun was returning to her convent from the market. A soldier on a motorcycle saw her and pulled over. Although she thought he stopped to help her with her heavy basket of food, she soon found out otherwise. As he forced her into the woods, she screamed, but no one heard her.

The trauma that occurred that day haunted her with nightmares for years, but gradually she began to heal. Years later, she was chosen to host a meeting of German teachers as a gesture of postwar reconciliation. Among them was her aggressor. It all came back! The bitterness and the thoughts of revenge were unbearable until she spent the night in prayer. Crying out to God, she eventually found the grace to serve them—all of them. She was finally free![2]

Until we forgive, we are the prisoner of the person who has offended or hurt us.

ONLY GOD VINDICATES

Sometimes we are minding our own business and pow! out of nowhere we are falsely accused of something. It's unfair. It's wrong, so what should we do? God's Word cautions us from trying to vindicate ourselves when others point the finger at us falsely. Instead, we should "drink the cup" and the Lord will defend us as illustrated in Numbers 5:11-20. In the Old Testament, a man who suspected his wife of adultery brought her to the priest where she was given dirty water to drink from a cup. If she was guilty, she would get sick and diseased and become a curse among her people, but if she was innocent, the Lord would vindicate her. She would be fruitful and bear children. Either way, she had to drink the cup! (See Numbers 5:11-22.)

God knows our hearts. He knows the truth. If satan uses someone to lie about us, it is tempting to lash out and try to prove our innocence; however, by "drinking the cup" in a spirit of humility and forgiveness, we are trusting God to be the vindicator.

Of course this does not mean that if someone makes a serious false accusation against us we should ignore it and hope it will go away. We can respond in a spirit of humility and address the false accusation, then we should lay it down and allow God to defend us. Our role needs to be one of forgiveness, otherwise we will harbor resentment.

Become Offense Proof

As much as we try to live peaceably, we will, now and again, offend others and they will offend us. Consequently, forgiveness is an enormous part of our daily lives. We may be insulted. Our feelings may be hurt. But we must not fall into the trap of unforgiveness when someone has offended us. In John 16:1 Jesus declared, "These things I have spoken to you that you should not be made to stumble [be offended]" (John 16:1 NKJV).

The word "offense" is a translation of a Greek word referring to the part of a trap to which the bait was attached in order to catch animals. For example, monkeys are trapped by bait that is placed in a cage. When the monkeys reach into the cage to take the bait, they can escape only by releasing the bait and running away. But they usually do not want to release the prize, so they end up being trapped. If they would only release the bait, they could go free. When we forgive and release those who have offended us, we also can go free. It is up to us!

Sometimes we are even tempted to take on a "borrowed offense." For example, perhaps I do or say something that offends my friend. He relates the incident to his wife. His wife is my coworker, so when she comes to work, she is mad at me! She is not the person to put the matter right, because the offense is not hers, but her husband's. She has picked up someone else's offense—her husband's!

The enemy uses offenses to bring people into captivity. Let's guard our hearts so that we will not look to give offense, nor look to find offense. Prayer and forgiveness are coupled together

(Matt. 6:9-15; Mark 11:24-26). Forgiving others is crucial to maintaining a healthy, intimate relationship with Jesus.

Forgiveness Is the Key

Forgiveness is the key to being restored to God's fellowship and being restored to others. When we "forgive the debts of others," we restore them to our fellowship just as God restores us to His fellowship when we ask for his forgiveness. It's a two way street. The petition of asking God to "forgive our debts, as we forgive our debtors" (Matt. 6:12) includes not only forgiveness; it also teaches us how to live with others.

Stormie Omartian, who experienced a traumatic childhood and subsequently experienced an enormous amount of the Lord's love and forgiveness, shares her story:

> "You're worthless, and you'll never amount to anything," my mother said as she pushed me into the little closet underneath the stairway and slammed the door....I felt lonely, unloved, and painfully afraid as I waited in that dark hole for the seemingly endless amount of time it took for her to remember I was there or for my father to return, at which time she would make sure I was let out.

> During all my growing-up years, my mother's extremely erratic behavior left me with feelings of futility, hopelessness, helplessness, and deep emotional pain.

> Many years later I sat in front of Mary Anne, a Christian counselor, who told me I needed to forgive my mother if I wanted to find complete wholeness and healing. Forgive someone who treated me with hatred and abuse? Someone who has ruined my life by making me into an emotional cripple? How can I? I thought to myself, overwhelmed at the prospect of so great a task...."You don't have to feel forgiveness in order to say you forgive someone," Mary Anne explained. "Forgiveness is something

you do out of obedience to the Lord because He has forgiven you." As difficult as it was, I did as Mary Anne said because I wanted to forgive my mother even though I felt nothing close to that at the time. "God, I forgive my mother," I said at the end of the prayer. I knew that for me even to be able to say those words, the power of God must be working in my life. And I felt His love at that moment more than I ever had before.[3]

That's What God's Forgiveness Can Do!

Bible teacher Joyce Meyer forgave her father for sexually abusing her as a child. She had the privilege of seeing him come to Christ and she had the opportunity to baptize her elderly father. The baptism followed Meyer's reaching out to her father in reconciliation and forgiveness.[4]

No longer feeling the pain of the hurts you have experienced from others may not happen overnight. It may be a process. We must keep our freedom by going into the freedom room each day to be sure we are not harboring unforgiveness. Corrie ten Boom, who along with her sister experienced life in a Nazi concentration camp, attested to the "ding-dong theory" when it came to finding complete healing and freedom. She said that when you make a decision to forgive someone and ask the Lord to heal and restore you, the devil will try to bring some of the old emotions of hurt and pain back to you again and again. But like the ding-dong of a church bell that rings loud at first and then grows softer and softer until it finally stops ringing, the hurts will grow more faint and distant as day by day you continue to declare your forgiveness of others and claim healing and restoration for your life.[5]

Turn Accusation Into Intercession

The enemy is an accuser, and there are five areas of accusation from which we must regularly find freedom. The devil accuses: us to God, God to us, us to others, others to us, and he even accuses us to ourselves (we often call this condemnation). In each area, we must learn to turn accusation into intercession in the freedom room. The Bible gives us this warning to protect us; "…judgment without mercy will be shown to anyone who has not been merciful. Mercy triumphs over judgment!" (James 2:13).

In other words, a merciful person rejoices in opportunities to show mercy rather than acting according to strict justice. Even though we have been hurt and want justice, if we forgive that person we are set free. If we harbor unforgiveness, it leads to a slow death.

Forgiveness is ongoing because once you've dealt with the past, constant infractions occur in the present. None of us gets by without having our pride wounded or being manipulated, offended, or hurt by someone. Each time that happens it leaves a scar on the soul if not confessed, released, and dealt with before the Lord. Besides that, unforgiveness also separates you from people you love. They sense a spirit of unforgiveness, even if they can't identify it, and it makes them uncomfortable and distant.[6]

R.T. Kendall, pastor and author of the book *Total Forgiveness* claims forgiveness is the greatest lesson he ever learned in all of his years as a minister and a Christian statesman. This is why we need to experience the freedom room each day. It is one thing to find freedom, it is another thing to stay free. The freedom room is for our protection, and this is our next room of prayer—the protection room.

THE FREEDOM ROOM
Apply what you've learned:

1. Describe a time a root of bitterness grew and you became a prisoner of the one who hurt you.

2. What does it mean to be offense proof?

3. Should we ignore a serious false accusation against us? Explain.

4. How has forgiveness taught you how to live with others?

For additional prayers, and an ever increasing intimate friendship with Jesus, see Chapter 9 in the Daily Prayer Guide.

ENDNOTES

1. W. Phillip Keller, *A Layman Looks at the Lord's Prayer* (Chicago, IL: Moody Press, 1976), 123.

2. Bible Study on Character—Forgiving One Another, http://www.swapmeetdave.com/Bible/Forgiving.htm (accessed January 2007).

3. Stormie Omartian, *Seven Prayers That Will Change Your Life Forever* (Nashville, TN: J. Countryman, a division of Thomas Nelson, Inc., 2006), 43-46.

4. "Joyce Meyer Forgives, Then Baptizes Father Who Sexually Abused Her," Charisma NewsService, http://www.connectionmagazine.org/2002_05/ts_joyce_meyer.htm (accessed January 2007).

5. Corrie ten Boom with James Buckingham, *Tramp for the Lord* (Grand Rapids, MI: Fleming H. Revell Company, Division of Baker Book House Co., 1974).

6. Stormie Omartian, *Seven Prayers That Will Change Your Life Forever* (Nashville: J. Countryman, a division of Thomas Nelson, Inc., 2006), 47-48.

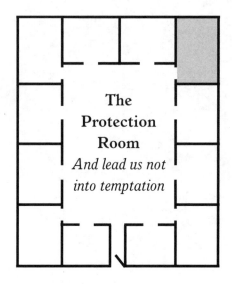

**The
Protection
Room**
*And lead us not
into temptation*

*If we do not abide in prayer,
we will abide in temptation. Let
this be one aspect of our daily
intercession: "God, preserve my
soul, and keep my heart and all
its ways so that I will not be
entangled." When this is true in
our lives, a passing temptation
will not overcome us. We will remain
free while others lie in bondage.*

—John Owen

CHAPTER 10

The Protection Room

AND LEAD US NOT INTO TEMPTATION

Everyone is tempted. Daily we are bombarded with self-centered desires. Most of us do not have to be reminded how easy it is to be enticed to follow our selfish desires. What can we do?

Jesus tells us to pray for God's help and victory. He told His disciples: "Pray that you may not enter into temptation" (Luke 22:40 NKJV). "The spirit indeed is willing, but the flesh is weak" (Matt. 26:41 NKJV). We need to pray every day for God's protection over our lives so we do not fall into sin. Temptation is something we enter into.

When we pray this prayer, we are essentially saying, "God, I ask You to lead me and carry me, so I do not fall into temptation. I depend totally on You to keep me from sin."

Jesus was tempted like we are. He was human and can identify with our struggles. He understands what it is like to be tempted:

> For we do not have a High Priest who cannot sympathize with our weaknesses, but was in all points tempted as we are, yet without sin. Let us therefore come boldly to the throne of grace, that we may obtain mercy and find grace to help in time of need" (Hebrews 4:15-16 NKJV).

We are vulnerable and open to attack; however, each temptation, or time of testing, is an opportunity to grow and find grace.

Don't Give In!

Being tempted, of course, is not sinning. Sin comes from yielding to temptation. When we ask God to lead us "not into temptation," we mean "do not allow us to enter" or "do not let us yield to" temptation. Sin only happens when we give in to temptation. "But each one is tempted when he is drawn away by his own desires and enticed. Then, when desire has conceived, it gives birth to sin; and sin, when it is full-grown, brings forth death" (James 1:14-15 NKJV).

Our minds are bombarded with many thoughts every day, some not from God. It is important to understand that temptation is not sin because every Christian is tempted. Temptation becomes sin when we think about it and begin to allow it to gain control of our thoughts and our actions.

We Pray About Temptations Because They Are Potentially Dangerous

Some time ago, a nursery in British Columbia had to track down people who bought poisonous plants that were incorrectly labeled "tasty in soup." The label should have read, "All parts of this plant are toxic," but an employee changed it to, "All parts of this plant are tasty in soup," as a practical joke. He thought it would be caught by a horticulturist. Sometimes our temptations seem to come labeled, "tasty in soup" even though in reality, they pose a great danger.[1] Temptation may come marked as something harmless that will do no harm when in actuality it has the potential to devastate lives if we yield to it.

We know that temptation does not come from God, but satan. "When tempted, no one should say, 'God is tempting me.' For God cannot be tempted by evil, nor does He tempt anyone" (James 1:13). Christ was tempted by satan: "And He was there in the wilderness forty days, tempted by satan" (Mark 1:13 NKJV). Paul was concerned that satan was tempting the Thessalonians: "I was afraid that the tempter had gotten the best of you and that our work had been useless" (1 Thess. 3:5 NLT).

So, we recognize we really need Jesus to help us resist those insidious things that pull us away from God. Prayer is essential in resisting temptation. If we pray and put our trust in the Word of God revealed in the Bible, He will be right there to help us resist temptation and stop us from allowing sin into our hearts and thoughts. He responds to us when we ask Him.

The Bible says, "Blessed is the man who endures temptation; for when he has been approved, he will receive the crown of life which the Lord has promised to those who love Him" (James 1:12 NKJV). As I have learned to enter the protection room day by day, I can sense God's power readily available to keep me from falling into the enemy's schemes.

God's Word also says that He provides a way out of temptation, "No temptation has seized you except what is common to man. And God is faithful; He will not let you be tempted beyond what you can bear. But when you are tempted, He will also provide a way out so that you can stand up under it" (1 Cor. 10:13). God will give us power in the midst of temptation to endure. He promises to give us the strength to resist temptation.

The path to victory over temptation is to admit defeat. We have to stop fighting it on our own power and come to God and make it a matter of prayer. It's when we stop trying to overcome the problem on our own that we begin to draw on God's power. With God's help, we can withstand temptation. God turns our weakness into strength. When we come to God in weakness and depend on Him in the protection room, we find His strength to help meet our needs.

God's Protection Promises Do Not Fall Short

The protection room is also a great place for us to pray for protection for our families and friends, for our spiritual leaders, our leaders in government and for missionaries. The Bible says, "For everything in the world—the cravings of sinful man, the lust of his eyes and the boasting of what he has and does—comes not from the Father but from the world" (1 John 2:16). According to this Scripture, the three main areas of temptation we all face are: (1) coveting—the cravings of sinful man, (2) lust—the lust of his eyes and (3) pride—the boasting of what he has and does. In the protection room, let's pray for the godly opposite: generosity, purity, and humility.

Take time to listen to the Holy Spirit. Receive the Lord's promises of protection here in the protection room. I encourage you to pray through Psalm 91, claiming each promise as your own and for those the Lord leads you to pray for.

> *He who dwells in the shelter of the Most High*
> *will rest in the shadow of the Almighty.*
> *I will say of the Lord, "He is my refuge and my fortress,*
> *my God, in whom I trust."*
> *Surely He will save you from the fowler's snare*
> *and from the deadly pestilence.*
> *He will cover you with His feathers,*
> *and under His wings you will find refuge;*
> *His faithfulness will be your shield and rampart.*
> *You will not fear the terror of night,*
> *nor the arrow that flies by day,*
> *nor the pestilence that stalks in the darkness,*
> *nor the plague that destroys at midday.*
> *A thousand may fall at your side,*
> *ten thousand at your right hand,*
> *but it will not come near you.*
> *You will only observe with your eyes*
> *and see the punishment of the wicked.*
> *If you make the Most High your dwelling—*
> *even the Lord, who is my refuge—*
> *then no harm will befall you,*
> *no disaster will come near your tent.*
> *For He will command His angels concerning you*

to guard you in all your ways;
they will lift you up in their hands,
so that you will not strike your foot against a stone.
You will tread upon the lion and the cobra;
you will trample the great lion and the serpent.
"Because He loves Me," says the Lord, "I will rescue him
I will protect him, for He acknowledges my name.
He will call upon Me, and I will answer him;
I will be with him in trouble,
I will deliver him and honor him.
With long life will I satisfy him
and show him my salvation" (Psalm 91).

Praying through Psalm 91 is not only for the purpose of focusing on our own protection from temptation and harm and danger. God is calling us to intercede for others in the protection room for their safety. Many times, while in the protection room, I have been impressed in prayer to pray for protection for a family member, for someone in our church, or for someone in another nation. Sometimes the Lord reveals to me later why he impressed me to pray, and at other times only eternity will give the details of the outcome of these prayers.

A few years ago, our sixteen-year-old daughter along with four friends were involved in an auto accident whereby their car was broad-sided by an eighteen wheeler traveling at 55 miles per hour. One girl's grandmother awakened at 11:20 p.m. and felt she should pray for the safety of her granddaughter. She obeyed and entered into the protection room in prayer. It turned out that this inner witness of the Holy Spirit nudged her to pray during the exact time of the accident. I truly believe that because she listened to God's still, small voice, and prayed, no one was hurt significantly in this potentially deadly accident.

Notice that Psalm 91 says God commands His angels to keep you safe! They have a special charge: They enforce God's promises to keep you from danger and harm.

So no matter where you are—at home, at school, at work, on vacation—God has promised to protect you. He will keep you from falling because His promises do not fall short! You can count on it.

Now let's press on to learn how to put on our spiritual armor as we enter into the warfare room with the commander in chief of the hosts of Heaven's armies, our Lord Jesus Christ.

THE PROTECTION ROOM
Apply what you've learned:

1. What can we do when we are tempted?

2. Share with someone an area of your life for which you need prayer to keep you from temptation.

3. What are some seemingly harmless temptations that can do great harm?

4. Describe a time the Lord protected you and kept you from falling into sin.

For additional prayers, and an ever increasing intimate friendship with Jesus, see Chapter 10 in the Daily Prayer Guide.

ENDNOTE

1. "Lead Us Not Into Temptation," www.dashhouse.com/sermons/2005 (accessed January 2007).

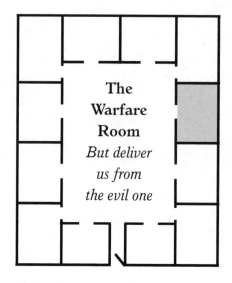

**The
Warfare
Room**
*But deliver
us from
the evil one*

*We must no longer see prayer as
preparation for action. Prayer must
be understood as action itself, a way
of responding, a potent spiritual
weapon to be used in spiritual
warfare against the most powerful
forces in the world. Prayer is not
undertaken instead of other actions,
but as a foundation for all the
rest of the actions we take.*

—Jim Wallis

CHAPTER 11

The Warfare Room

BUT DELIVER US FROM THE EVIL ONE

Life is not easy. It is a daily battle. It's a life and death battle to the finish with the devil. In the previous room, we prayed for Jesus to keep us from failing when we are tested. So here in the warfare room, we ask God to deliver us from the evil one who wants us to fail.

As Christians, we are engaged in a spiritual conflict with evil. Although we have been guaranteed victory through Christ's death on the cross, we must wage spiritual warfare by the power of the Holy Spirit. (See Romans 8:13.)

Spiritual warfare is real. The Scriptures teach us:

...though we live in the world, we do not wage war as the world does. The weapons we fight with are not the weapons of the world. On the contrary, they have divine power to demolish strongholds. We demolish arguments and every pretension that sets itself up against the knowledge of God, and we take captive every thought to make it obedient to Christ (2 Corinthians 10:3-5).

And much of this warfare happens daily in our minds, as we "take every thought captive" and learn from Scripture to think like God thinks.

Paul, the apostle, commanded us to "fight the good fight of faith" (1 Tim. 6:12). The devil is trying to devour us like a roaring lion (see 1 Pet. 5:8) or deceive us disguised as an angel of light (see

2 Cor. 11:14). If we don't learn to fight we are in trouble. We must continually fight against those things that limit God's work in our lives.

Prayer is our communication line with God. During war, if a battalion loses contact with headquarters, the soldiers are in serious trouble, becoming much more vulnerable to the enemy. It often works the same way in our Christian lives. We are in a spiritual war. The devil is constantly trying to break down our communication line with God.

How does a Christian wage war? The Scriptures exhort us to be strong in the Lord and put on the whole armor of God so we are properly prepared to engage in our spiritual conflict with evil. Paul tells us to put on spiritual armor like a soldier does so we can stand against satan's schemes:

> *Finally, be strong in the Lord and in His mighty power. Put on the full armor of God so that you can take your stand against the devil's schemes. For our struggle is not against flesh and blood, but against the rulers, against the authorities, against the powers of this dark world and against the spiritual forces of evil in the heavenly realms* (Ephesians 6:10-12).

Our fight is not with people; the real war is with the demons of hell, the angels of darkness. The only weapons to which they respond are spiritual weapons. Prayer is a powerful spiritual weapon against the powers of darkness. And remember, it is not us against the devil, it is *us and God* against the devil!

PUT ON GOD'S ARMOR

In Tolkien's story, *The Lord of the Rings*, an interesting character is that of the irresponsible and careless young hobbit, Pippin, who never intended to be heroic, but went on to become a knight of Gondor, literally in shining armor. He started out as a timid hobbit, but rose to meet the greatest of challenges. Like Pippin, God can take the weakest and most insignificant of us and make us strong when we put on the armor of God.

In Ephesians, we are instructed as to why we should put on the armor of God:

> *Therefore put on the full armor of God, so that when the day of evil comes, you may be able to stand your ground, and after you have done everything, to stand. Stand firm then, with the belt of truth buckled around your waist, with the breastplate of righteousness in place, and with your feet fitted with the readiness that comes from the Gospel of peace. In addition to all this, take up the shield of faith, with which you can extinguish all the flaming arrows of the evil one. Take the helmet of salvation and the sword of the Spirit, which is the word of God. And pray in the Spirit on all occasions with all kinds of prayers and requests. With this in mind, be alert and always keep on praying for all the saints* (Ephesians 6:13-18).

God has called us to stand firm in the midst of attacks from the enemy. As Christians, we are in a constant fight with the desires of our sinful natures. We are in steady need of God's guidance so that our needs and desires are kept in proper balance. It has been my experience that most spiritual failure happens when Christians fail to keep their spiritual armor in place.

When you get up in the morning, declare that your armor is in place. Proclaim that you have placed the belt of truth around your waist. You are righteous through faith in Jesus Christ; the breastplate is in place. Affirm that you have peace with God through your Lord Jesus Christ (see Rom. 5:1) because you are justified through faith. Declare that you will walk in complete forgiveness toward anyone who's hurt you, and that you have pursued peace with them as much as possible (see Rom. 12:18). Announce that you have taken up the shield of faith and will not allow the fiery darts of the enemy to hurt you. You will quench them in Jesus' name through faith in the word of God. Assert that your helmet of salvation is secure. You know you are born again and that Jesus Christ has changed your life.

When this passage refers to the Word of God, it actually uses the Greek word *rhema* of God, rather than the *logos* of God. Logos refers to the whole counsel of God and the whole of His word; *rhema* refers to a very specific word for a given situation. In warfare, therefore, we are not to brandish the word of God indiscriminately, but we are to find the very specific word for that situation, and use that as an offensive weapon to cause the enemy to flee.

With all the above, you can pray as a soldier who has properly placed on the armor that the Lord Jesus has given.

You are ready for action! The world around us is waiting for us to declare the truth that will set them free. With our armor in place, we can stand and declare, "He is my refuge and my fortress, my God, in whom I trust" (Ps. 91:2). We can trust that God will protect our lives and our loved ones' lives from temptation and harm.

BINDING STRONGHOLDS IN PEOPLE'S LIVES

Satan blinds the minds of people who do not believe. "And even if our Gospel is veiled, it is veiled to those who are perishing. The god of this age has blinded the minds of unbelievers, so that they cannot see the light of the Gospel..." (2 Cor. 4:3-4). Those who do not submit themselves to Jesus are under satan's rule. He "veils" their eyes to the truth of the Gospel to keep them from believing in Jesus Christ.

Imagine driving down a road and seeing a sign alerting you that a bridge is washed out. You immediately know you should follow the detour. Now imagine a drunk driver seeing the same sign. With his impaired judgment, he may read the sign without truly comprehending the dangers. It is possible he may drive off the edge of the bridge to his destruction because he was blinded to the truth. People all around us today are going to hell.

The Bible makes it clear that we can pray and bind the powers of darkness in Jesus' name, so that people will see the truth. Matthew 18:18 says, "I tell you the truth, whatever you bind on earth will be bound in Heaven, and whatever you loose on earth will be loosed in Heaven."

This verse is not some magic formula whereby our words alone control the spirit realm, and which we can pray indiscriminately, but it reveals to us a powerful authority Christ gives us to declare what he is doing and has already done. A very literal translation given in some versions is "whatever you bind on earth, will have been bound in Heaven," thus showing us that we must first be led by the Spirit to see what Christ is wanting to accomplish in a situation and then pray in His name according to His will that it be done. With such a Christ initiated prayer we have great authority to bind the work of the enemy. As the Holy Spirit leads us, we pray and bind the strongholds in peoples' lives so that they will be free to hear the Gospel and respond to Jesus Christ.

A young man once told me, "The only reason I am a Christian today is because my mother prayed for me." This mother understood the principles of the Kingdom of God. Let's get serious about praying for those whom the Lord has placed in our lives and who need to draw closer to Jesus. We can bind the blinding spirits deceiving them so that they can understand and respond to the good news of Jesus Christ.

WE CAN BE VICTORIOUS

The Bible says, "We are more than conquerors through Him who loved us" (Rom. 8:37). One time, after I spoke at a conference in Bulgaria, I was introduced to a world-renowned mid-weight boxer who had never lost a fight. I shook his hand and decreed, "You are a conqueror!" His wife, standing next to him, smiled when I turned to her and said, "And you are *more* than a conqueror."

"It's like this," I explained, "he does the fighting and gives you the money!" In the end, she had the complete victory— including the spoils of war!

You, too, can have the complete victory. As Christians, we need to realize that we can have victory in every area of our lives! This victory is promised in the first book of the Bible when God promises to redeem the world, giving us the victory over satan. Jesus came to earth to deliver us from satan's dominion and establish God's Kingdom in our hearts. He came to give us life and victory! The devil was defeated when Jesus died on the cross and rose from the dead two thousand years ago. Jesus helps us to come through every obstacle victoriously. We are more than conquerors through Christ!

Learn to fight for your family and for your spiritual sons and daughters (see Neh. 4:14). My friend Trevor Yaxley, an evangelist and entrepreneur from New Zealand, often says, "We must learn to enjoy the fight. We are told by Paul the apostle that we fight the good fight of faith. It is a good fight, because we win!"

Resist the devil, and he will flee from you (James 4:7-8).

I was driving down the road in my car one day when a spirit of fear came on me like a cloud. I was paralyzed with fear. Immediately I was aware of what was happening. The enemy was trying to cause me to live by my feelings of fear rather than doing the things I knew God was calling me to do. I said boldly, "In Jesus' name, I renounce this spirit of fear and command it to leave." And guess what? It left! When we resist the devil, he has to flee (see James 4:7)!

A few years ago, I was in Europe and experienced a similar spirit of fear. Again, this spirit of fear had to leave when confronted with the name of Jesus. We do not have to put up with a spirit of fear or any other affliction that the devil will try to bring against us. Jesus Christ has come to set us free!

RESISTING THE DEVIL

To be set free from demonic bondage we must resist the devil by prayer and proclaim God's Word as we call upon the mighty name of Jesus. A friend told me he once sensed a strange, evil presence at a friend's house. Calling upon the name of Jesus Christ, a few Christian believers prayed and took authority over a curse that needed to be broken over that home. The evil presence left.

Smith Wigglesworth was an evangelist in Great Britain years ago. He compared the devil to a stray dog that is barking at our heels. He taught that unless we resist the dog, he will continue with his "yelping" and aggravation. But if we boldly tell him to leave us alone, he will flee. The devil has no choice when we resist him in Jesus' name. He must flee.

As Christians, we can call upon Jesus to overcome satan and his demonic powers. Matthew 12:29-30 says we can tie up the strong man (satan) and rob his house (set free those who are enslaved to satan). "… How can anyone enter a strong man's house and carry off his possessions unless he first ties up the strong man? Then he can rob his house" (Matt. 12:29-30).

We can drive demons out in the name of Jesus by "tying up" the demonic spirit that is influencing our lives or someone else's life. Only then can we be free. As believers, we can provide deliverance for those who have been held captive by satan's power. "And these signs will accompany those who believe: In my name they will drive out demons…" (Mark 16:17).

I have a friend who parks his car outside the homes of people who are struggling spiritually. He often does this in the middle of the night and prays and fights for them in the spirit. He has learned to walk in the power of Christ that we can experience each day in the warfare room!

A lady recently told me she was in her home and an evil presence came into the room. She was terrified. Immediately she began to say, "Jesus, Jesus…" until the evil presence left. There is power in Jesus' name. His name is above every name!

Some may prefer to call this room the deliverance room (deliver us from evil). But whether you call it the warfare room or the deliverance room, remember: The reason the Son of God appeared was to destroy the devil's work (see 1 John 3:8-9). As Christians, we purpose in our hearts that we will not do that which Christ came to destroy. Jesus came to dissolve the power and influence of sin in our lives. We will not allow sin and evil to overtake us. We will instead allow Him to build His Kingdom in us. Let's go into the Kingdom room next.

THE WARFARE ROOM
Apply what you've learned:

1. How have you fought against something that limited God's work in your life?

2. Tell of a time you "put on" a specific piece of armor and used it as an offensive weapon to cause the enemy to flee.

3. Explain what it means to bring every thought captive to the obedience of Christ.

4. Have you ever prayed to bind a stronghold in someone's life? Explain.

For additional prayers, and an ever increasing intimate friendship with Jesus, see Chapter 11 in the Daily Prayer Guide.

The
Kingdom
Room
*For Yours is
the Kingdom*

*There is no way that Christians,
in a private capacity, can do
so much to promote the work
of God and advance the
Kingdom of Christ as by prayer.*

—Jonathan Edwards

CHAPTER 12

The Kingdom Room

FOR YOURS IS THE KINGDOM

As Christians, you and I are citizens of the Kingdom of God. It's a Kingdom that belongs to the Lord, and we are His sons and daughters. My friend Peter from Great Britain, who serves on our international leadership team, clearly understands "kingdoms." As a British citizen, he is a subject of a kingdom, with the present sovereign being Queen Elizabeth II. Christians live as citizens of the Kingdom of God, and as subjects of this Kingdom, we receive the benefits of Kingdom living.

"Yours is the Kingdom" refers not as much to the place where God rules as to the presence and power of God's actual rule. As God exercises His authority on earth, the Kingdom of God is here. Jesus proclaimed, "The time is fulfilled, and *the Kingdom of God has come near*; repent, and believe in the good news" (Mark 1:15 HCSB, emphasis added). When we recognize God's rule over our lives, we take on values that are fundamentally different than those of the world. Thus we make an about turn; we repent and live our lives in a new direction, pointing toward God's Kingdom.

What does it mean to be a child of the King, a citizen of the Kingdom? Charles Sheldon wrote a little book called *In His Steps* describing a group of Christians who decide to take seriously the claims of Jesus Christ on their lives. They try to live out their faith in practical ways, so they apply a test to all of their decisions and behavior. When they are faced with decisions or with issues of behavior, they agree to ask themselves the question, "What would

Jesus do?" Not surprisingly, as a result of asking themselves that question, their behavior begins to change and they begin to make a difference for Jesus Christ in their world.[1]

Like Jesus, both our words and our works should declare the reality of the Kingdom. We live out this reign each day by living as an active member of the community of Jesus—loving our enemies, forgiving those who wrong us, healing the sick, feeding the hungry, and confronting sin.

DECLARE THAT THE KINGDOM IS THE LORD'S!

As citizens of God's Kingdom, we have the privilege to come before the King of kings and Lord of lords, to enjoy communion with our Father who has blessed us in the heavenly realms with every spiritual blessing in Christ Jesus. He has chosen us before the creation of the world, predestined us to be adopted as His sons and daughters, redeemed us and revealed great things to us (see Eph. 1:3-8). God is excited about His Kingdom!

The "Kingdom room" is a place to declare, "Yours is the Kingdom!" When we declare it, we build up our confidence in God and His authority in the world and in our lives. Ultimate victory is ours through our sovereign Lord God Almighty! God in Christ has broken into the world to establish His sovereignty and defeat the powers of satan.

No matter what you are going through or how shaky you may feel during this stage of your life, you must know that you are a part of a Kingdom that cannot be shaken! The Scriptures teach us; "Therefore, since we are receiving a Kingdom that cannot be shaken, let us be thankful, and so worship God acceptably with reverence and awe, for our 'God is a consuming fire'" (Heb. 12:28-29). Thank God that no matter what is going on in your life at this moment; you are a vital part of His eternal Kingdom that cannot be shaken! Isn't that great news!

The word *kingdom* is weakened if we do not see and believe that we are representatives of the Lord's unshakeable Kingdom right here, on the earth. The Kingdom of God is within us (see

Luke 17:20-21). Everywhere you go, you take the Kingdom of God with you. God has made the resources of Heaven available to meet our needs here on earth when we pray in faith, believing that God will do what He has promised to do for His children.

Remember, the Kingdom of God is not a matter of eating and drinking, but of righteousness, peace, and joy in the Holy Spirit (see Rom. 14:17). Wherever there is a lack of righteousness, peace, and joy in the Holy Spirit, there is a lack of His Kingdom. If we see this lack in ourselves or in others—a lack of the kind of wholeness and peace in which God designed us to live—we can pray for His Kingdom to become more of a reality day by day in our lives and in the lives of those around us.

God's Kingdom includes every church and ministry on the face of the earth: past, present, and future. We need to keep this in perspective. God is not all that impressed with your church, whether it is an average-sized community church, a large megachurch, or a small house church. He is, however, excited about His Kingdom. His Kingdom includes all of His people in your region and the world who name the name of Jesus Christ and are committed to local expressions of the Body of Christ of many types and flavors. *Kingdom* however, is far more than the church—it is where the love of God is shown to the world; it is where the hungry are fed and the sick healed; it is where the arts or media or business reflect God to the world and are used to advance Kingdom values. All of these things help increase the presence of the heavenly Kingdom here on earth.

Pray Kingdom Prayers

Kingdom praying is praying for things that matter for eternity. It is being concerned about the things that God is concerned about. God intends that all believers everywhere expand His Kingdom through the work of prayer and intercession.

Paul, the apostle, admonishes and urges us to pray for all men, nations, and kingdoms.

I urge, then, first of all, that requests, prayers, intercession and thanksgiving be made for everyone—for kings and all those in authority, that we may live peaceful and quiet lives in all godliness and holiness (1 Timothy 2:1-2).

In the Kingdom room you can pray for your family, your business, your church, and your job. Pray that loved ones will find Jesus. Pray for restored marriages. Pray that you will have a hunger for God. Pray for healing and that people are delivered from oppression. Pray that the gifts of the Spirit will be developed in your life and in the lives of those around you.

Another Kingdom prayer that I pray each day is for the peace of Jerusalem, "Pray for the peace of Jerusalem: May those who love You be secure" (Ps. 122:6). God's purposes being fulfilled in Jerusalem is vital. We are not instructed in Scripture to pray for any other city. Jerusalem is on the Lord's heart.

Pray that your president or prime minister will have wisdom from God. Pray that spiritual leaders will walk in wisdom and be the people of prayer that God has called them to be. Be specific in your prayers, naming your town or city, your state, or province and the leader of your nation. Intercede for your nation. Pray for revival. Living in true revival and living in the Kingdom are one and the same.

When I enter the Kingdom room each morning, I often pray for the church of my region, including churches and ministries of many denominations. I pray that we may be one, as the Father and the Son are one (see John 17:21). God's Kingdom is characterized by unity. We can pray for unity between churches and spiritual leaders in our city or county. This is Kingdom praying.

I learned from two pastors in Dallas, Texas, 25 years ago that Isaiah 43 can be turned into a powerful prayer:

Do not be afraid, for I am with you; I will bring your children from the east and gather you from the west. I will say to the north, 'Give them up!' and to the south, 'Do not hold them back.' Bring My sons from afar and My daughters from the

ends of the earth—everyone who is called by My name, whom
I created for My glory, whom I formed and made (Isaiah
43:5-7).

In light of this Scripture, I have prayed both alone and with
others hundreds of times as I have spoken to the area north of my
town, "North, you have people God wills to become a part of the
Kingdom of God. Release every person to come into the Kingdom
of God and become a part of our church or another local church in
our community." Then we speak to the South, East, and West, and
in Jesus' name, also ask God to dispatch angels to minister to care
for people who will inherit salvation from these areas (see Heb.
1:13-14).

Kingdom praying is not just about our fulfillment, but our
transformation and the transformation of those around us. In this
way, we will witness the Kingdom being built as God transforms
lives.

Thousands of years ago the psalmist declared:

"All You have made will praise You, O Lord; Your saints will
extol You. They will tell of the glory of Your Kingdom and
speak of Your might, so that all men may know of Your mighty
acts and the glorious splendor of Your Kingdom. Your King-
dom is an everlasting Kingdom, and Your dominion endures
through all generations…" (Psalm 145:10-13).

"For the Kingdom is the Lord's" (Ps. 22:28 NKJV) declared
the psalmist, and Jesus said, "Do not be afraid, little flock, for your
Father has been pleased to give you the Kingdom" (Luke 12:32).
Paul also taught that we are partakers in God's Kingdom. "Giving
thanks to the Father, who has qualified you to share in the inheritance of the saints in the Kingdom of light" (Col. 1:12).

To Timothy, Paul declared, "The Lord will rescue me from
every evil attack and will bring me safely to His heavenly Kingdom" (2 Tim. 4:18). When we pray "yours is the Kingdom" we can
praise the Lord that He has rescued us and brought us into His

Kingdom of light. God has invited us to be participants in His Kingdom.

Prayer is the backbone of His Kingdom. Prayer is power. Prayer is probably one of the greatest contributions we can make to advance the Kingdom of Christ because it produces powerful results. God's Kingdom is characterized by His power. Let's take a few steps and enter into the next room—the power room.

THE KINGDOM ROOM
Apply what you've learned:

1. How did your values and behavior change when you recognized God's rule over your life and that you are a part of His unshakeable Kingdom?

2. What does it mean to you to be a child of the King, a citizen of the Kingdom?

3. How are you a representative of the Kingdom here on earth?

4. Do you see a lack of righteousness, peace, and joy in your life? This is a lack of His Kingdom. Pray Kingdom prayers for transformation in your life and other's lives.

For additional prayers, and an ever increasing intimate friendship with Jesus, see Chapter 12 in the Daily Prayer Guide.

ENDNOTE

1. Charles Sheldon, *In His Steps* (North Brunswick, NJ: Bridge-Logo Publishers, 1999).

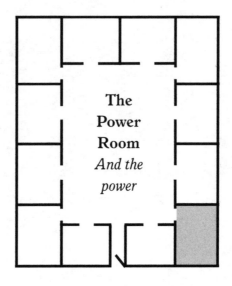

**The
Power
Room**
And the

power

*Where there is much prayer, there
will be much of the Spirit; where
there is much of the Spirit, there will
be ever-increasing prayer.*

—Andrew Murray

CHAPTER 13

The Power Room

AND THE POWER

A man who lived in a poor village in the interior of his nation had the opportunity to travel to a large city. Having never experienced the use of electricity before, he was fascinated when he saw electric light bulbs for the first time. He asked his host if he could have one to take back to his home. When he got back to his village, he hung the light bulb on a string in his hut. He was frustrated because it wouldn't work, until someone explained to him that it had to be plugged into a power source.

To enter into the fullness of what God has planned for our lives, we have no greater need than to be plugged into the power source of the Holy Spirit. We desperately need the Holy Spirit's power operating in our lives: "For the Kingdom of God is not a matter of talk but of power" (1 Cor. 4:20).

PRAY IN THE SPIRIT

As we enter the "power room" we begin to pray for a new dimension of the Holy Spirit's power in our lives and in the lives of those we are praying for.

Pray with unceasing prayer and entreaty on every fitting occasion in the Spirit, and be always on the alert to seize opportunities for doing so, with unwearied persistence and entreaty on behalf of all God's people" (Ephesians 6:18 Weymouth).

We desperately need the power of God to be manifested in our lives. A young man in Redding, California, went to the 24-hour grocery store one evening to buy some doughnuts. The girl attending the cash register was wearing a hearing aid. The young man asked if he could pray for her, and she said "yes." She was immediately healed. The young man felt there was a presence of God in the store to heal that evening so he asked if he could use the store intercom to see if others might respond to his announcement offering prayer. He was granted permission and let people know he was up front praying for the sick. Numerous people responded that evening and were healed. The young man said he never did get his doughnuts—more important power encounters were taking place!

With the power of God evident in our lives, we are empowered to minister to others. Even after Jesus had breathed on His disciples and told them to "receive the Holy Spirit," He made it clear that their experience was still incomplete. In His final words to them before His ascension, He commanded them not to go out and preach immediately, but to go back to Jerusalem and wait there until they were baptized in the Holy Spirit and thus given the power they needed to be effective witnesses (see Acts 1:4-5,8). So the disciples prayed and waited. During the festival of Pentecost, 120 of His disciples were gathered together in one place, and it happened! Here, the disciples experienced the mighty infilling of the Holy Spirit. To enter into the fullness of what God has planned for our lives, we have no greater need than to be plugged into the power source. We need the mighty infilling of the Holy Spirit. It is the gateway into a new dimension of the Spirit's presence and power in our lives, and it empowers us for ministry.

Praying with power can take various forms. We can pray in the language we speak (English, Spanish, Swahili, French, for example) or speak in spiritual languages (our prayer language between us and God used to build us up spiritually). Paul is referring to both when he describes how he prays in First Corinthians 14:15: "I will pray with my spirit, but I will also pray with my mind" (1 Cor. 14:5). If we sincerely desire to rise above our limitations and look to God, a new inner strength becomes ours by the power of the Holy Spirit.

Oswald Chambers said that God's purpose for us is "that we depend on Him and His power now." By depending on God's power instead of our own, we are fulfilling God's purpose for our lives. God's power is a gift to be used to heal us in our inner beings. He can "strengthen you with power through His Spirit in your inner being" (Eph. 3:16). We simply pray for His power and receive it from Him.

POWER OF PRAYER

The king in Shakespeare's "Hamlet" fails miserably in prayer. In explanation, he says: "My words fly up, my thoughts remain below, words without thoughts never to Heaven go." We, too, fail if our prayers are "words without thoughts" that remain earthbound because they are only words we say. Praying is not about saying the right words. Rather, the power of prayer comes from the Holy Spirit inside us helping us to pray earnest prayers.

The power of prayer cannot be underestimated. James 5:16 declares, "…The prayer of a righteous man is powerful and effective." When we pray purposefully, God responds powerfully! So, as you pray in the power room, give praise to the Father because He has made His power available to you:

> *Yours, O Lord, is the greatness and the power and the glory and the majesty and the splendor, for everything in Heaven and earth is yours. Yours, O Lord, is the Kingdom; You are exalted as head over all* (1 Chronicles 29:11).

> *Be strong in the Lord and in His mighty power* (Ephesians 6:10).

When we approach God, He wants us to trust Him fully and understand that only He has the solutions to our problems. We can't solve them on our own. It is this recognition that releases the power of God. In prayer, we are expressing that commitment and trust we have in God.

In the power room we give God full control of a situation. We acknowledge that He is sovereign in that area. As a result, God begins to work on the problem with His mighty power. John Wesley said, "God does everything by prayer and nothing without it." In the power room, give praise to your Father for allowing you to be a participant in His power and for making His power available to you.

In Acts chapter 4, the early church met together to cry out to God for His power to be manifested. And God responded to their prayers. The building shook and they were filled with the Holy Spirit and spoke the word of God with boldness. These were many of the same disciples who were filled with the Holy Spirit in Acts chapter 2. They were filled with the Holy Spirit again. Power in our lives does not just happen. It comes in response to prayer. If you desire to learn more about being filled with the Holy Spirit, I encourage you to read a booklet I wrote on being filled with the Spirit.[1]

As you meet with God in the power room each day, you can be a participant in His power because His power is available to you. God told Zerubbabel that man's weakness is no obstacle for God. "Not by might nor by power, but by My Spirit..." (Zech. 4:6). We can trust that God's mighty power will break through to bring healing, change hearts, heal emotional wounds, grant wisdom, defeat demons, and change a myriad of other situations when we pray in the power room. We are drawing on the might of the infinitely powerful God of the universe. May He be exalted!

THE POWER ROOM
Apply what you've learned:

1. Do you feel you have entered into the fullness of what God has planned for your life?

2. Pray for a new dimension of the Holy Spirit's power in your life today.

3. Describe a time you felt empowered to minister to another person.

4. Tell of a time God's power broke through to bring healing, changed someone's heart, or gave wisdom.

For additional prayers, and an ever increasing intimate friendship with Jesus, see Chapter 13 in the Daily Prayer Guide.

ENDNOTE

1. Larry Kreider, *How Can I Be Filled with the Holy Spirit?* (Lititz, PA: House to House Publications, 2006).

The
Exaltation
Room
*And the glory
forever. Amen.*

*Prayer is not a convenient device
for imposing our will upon God,
or bending His will to ours,
but the prescribed way of
subordinating our will to His.*

—John R. W. Stott

CHAPTER 14

The Exaltation Room

AND THE GLORY FOREVER. AMEN.

We begin our journey to become a house of prayer with "our Father" and we end it by "glorifying our Father." The last room in the house of prayer is the exaltation room. The ambiance of this room is unbeatable. I imagine it as a bright, dazzling sunroom with glass on all sides radiating sunlight and energy.

Exalting God is giving Him all the glory and praise that only He deserves! We worship Him and Him alone. Our highest desire is for Jesus Christ to be honored and glorified.

"Who is this King of glory?" asked the psalmist. The answer: "The Lord strong and mighty, the Lord mighty in battle" (Ps. 24:8). "Glory and honor are in His presence" (1 Chron. 16:27 KJV). God Himself declares: "I am the Lord: That is My name: and My glory will I not give to another, neither My praise to graven images" (Isa. 42:8). What is God's glory?

When the Bible speaks of the glory of God it is referring to His worth and honor and greatness. Or, when this word is used of God, we could say that His majesty or supremacy is in view.

All of creation has as its goal and purpose the glory of God. He created everything for His own glory. Everything that exists has its existence from God and for God. Romans 11:36 says, "For from Him and through Him and to Him are all things. To Him be the glory forever!"[1]

Because God is glorious and perfect, our worship focuses on who God is—on His person. We thank Him because He is God. Everyone worships something. Some people worship themselves. Some people worship their jobs, a motorcycle, sports, or a spouse. We have been chosen to worship only God. The word *worship* comes from an old Anglo-Saxon word, *weorthsceipe*, which means "to ascribe worth to our God." Only God is worthy of glory and praise. The Bible says in John 4:23-24 that we must worship with our heart. It cannot be merely form because "…true worshipers will worship the Father in spirit and truth, for they are the kind of worshipers the Father seeks. God is spirit, and His worshipers must worship in spirit and in truth."

Louie Giglio, in his book *The Air I Breathe*, says:

> Worship should matter to you because it matters to God. And worship matters to God because He knows he's worthy. I know that doesn't sound too persuasive in our me-centered culture, but it's true. Worship doesn't begin with us. Worship begins and ends with God. And God is worthy of all praise, from all people, for all time.[2]

The tabernacle of David in the Old Testament was known as a place of freedom in praise and worship. God is going to rebuild the tabernacle of David again in the last days (Acts 15:16). That is why God is bringing the freedom to worship to His Church today.

Music is a basic form of worship. Music was so important in David's day that he appointed people with instruments to praise and worship the Lord (1 Chron. 15:16;16:5-6). God's original intention of unbridled praise and worship is being restored to His Church today.

We need to be involved privately in praise and worship to our God in our time alone with Him. In the same way that the moon reflects the glory of the sun, we will reflect the glory of God in our lives as we spend time worshiping Him. The Book of Psalms is filled with songs of praise to our God. I encourage you to take the

Book of Psalms and begin to sing those psalms and make up your own songs and use them to give worship to God.

Prepare for Heaven!

We praise and worship and exalt the Lord here on earth in preparation for Heaven. Some day we will all stand before the Lord and honor and glorify Him, but we can begin today. The Bible says that earth is the place in which to praise the Lord for His mercies, and to prepare for His glory. "It is not the dead who praise the Lord, those who go down to silence" (Ps. 115:17).

Although I am not an exceptionally emotional person, when I realize what Jesus Christ did for me, my spirit, soul, and body begin to get caught up in praise and worship to my God. According to the Scripture, the demons of hell can be bound (tied up spiritually) through praise and worship to our God. Psalm 149:6-8 says, "May the praise of God be in their mouths and a double-edged sword in their hands, to inflict vengeance on the nations and punishment on the peoples, to bind their kings with fetters, their nobles with shackles of iron" (Ps. 149:6-8).

Whether we are alone or with two or three others or with one thousand people, the demons tremble when God's people commune with Him through praise and worship. God inhabits, actually lives in, the praises of His people. "But You are holy, enthroned in the praises of Israel" (Ps. 22:3 NKJV).

Expressing Worship

There are so many ways that we can express worship and praise to our God. Here are just a few of the ways mentioned in the Scriptures. In the exaltation room, feel free to express yourself!

First of all, we can kneel before the Lord. "Come, let us bow down in worship, let us kneel before the Lord our Maker" (Ps. 95:6).

We can stand and worship our God like the multitude of people in Revelation:

"A great multitude that no one could count, from every nation, tribe, people and language, standing before the throne and in front of the Lamb. They were wearing white robes and were holding palm branches in their hands. And they cried out in a loud voice: "Salvation belongs to our God, who sits on the throne, and to the Lamb" (Revelation 7:9-10).

The Scripture also says there are times God has called us to lift up our hands to the Lord. "I want men everywhere to lift up holy hands in prayer..." (1 Tim. 2:8).

Other Scriptures teach us we should be still before the Lord. "Be still, and know that I am God..." (Ps. 46:10).

We are also exhorted to praise Him with instruments. "Praise Him with the sounding of the trumpet, praise Him with the harp and lyre...praise Him with the clash of cymbals, praise Him with resounding cymbals" (Ps. 150:3,5).

The children of Israel loved to worship God through dancing. Many of God's people today also worship the Lord in dance. The word dance in Hebrew means "the lifting of the feet." David danced before the Lord in the Old Testament. The devil has taken dance and made it sensual, but God is restoring dance to His Church in purity through praise and worship to our King Jesus. Psalm 149:3 says, "Let them praise His name with dancing and make music to Him with tambourine and harp."

God has also called us to sing new songs to our God. Singing a new song is simply asking God to give us a tune or a melody and then allowing the Holy Spirit to give us the words. Or we can take the words directly from the Scriptures and sing them to Him. "Praise the Lord. Sing to the Lord a new song, His praise in the assembly of the saints" (Ps. 149:1). Singing alone in God's presence is a fresh way to minister to the Lord.

The Scripture also speaks of clapping and shouting unto the Lord. Remember the time God's people marched around Jericho day after day? On the seventh day, the walls came tumbling down (Josh. 6:15-16,20). Demons tremble when we shout because of what Jesus Christ has done and because of who He is. The Bible says we should clap and shout with cries of joy. "Clap your hands, all you nations; shout to God with cries of joy" (Ps. 47:1).

Ephesians 5:19 says that we should be speaking to one another in psalms and hymns and spiritual songs and making melody in our hearts to the Lord. Our God wants us to have communion with Him and relationship with Him. Sometimes we express that relationship by being quiet and listening. Sometimes we sing unto our God. We've been created to praise and commune with our wonderful, heavenly Daddy. Sing along with your favorite worship CD and bask in the Lord's presence.

God will invade our lives and the devil is defeated when we sing alone in His presence. Mary Slosser, who worked in China for many years, used to say, "I sing the Doxology and dismiss the devil." And Amy Carmichael said, "I believe truly that satan cannot endure it and so slips out of the room—more or less—when there is a true song."[3]

Singing to the Lord during prayer can be a weapon of warfare. When the children of Judah found themselves outnumbered by hostile armies, the people sought the Lord for His help. The Lord assured them that He would fight for them. Knowing that God manifests His power through praise, the people of Judah sent their army against their enemies, led by the praisers. The Bible says, "As they began to sing and praise, the Lord set ambushes against the men of Ammon and Moab and Mount Seir who were invading Judah, and they were defeated" (2 Chron. 20:22).

When you praise the Lord, the enemy takes flight. Praising God and becoming a person of praise will cause a release of the power of God in your life. The enemies of God are thrown into confusion by the songs of God's people. God takes our offering of praise and makes it an occasion for His power to be manifested. So sing with all your heart. God will ambush the devil!

MAGNIFY GOD

As we come to these final moments of prayer, let's pause to contemplate our awesome God. Our God is able to "do immeasurably more than all we ask or imagine, according to His power that is at work within us" (Eph. 3:20). The exaltation room is the place to expand our vision of God and to give Him the honor and glory that only He deserves.

Martin Luther said this about the conclusion of the Lord's Prayer:

> Never doubt you are alone in your prayer. Do not leave your prayer without having said or thought, "Very well, God has heard my prayer, this I know as a certainty and a truth." This is what Amen means.[4]

"Amen" illustrates something is said that is of absolute certainty. You can leave your house of prayer knowing without a doubt that your God has heard and is answering your prayers.

The Exaltation Room
Apply what you've learned:

1. Describe a time of worship that was especially meaningful to you.

2. How has singing to the Lord during prayer ever been a weapon of warfare for you?

3. Are you finding complete freedom in worship? Explain.

4. Take some time to worship God in a way you don't normally worship Him. Move out of your comfort zone!

For additional prayers, and an ever increasing intimate friendship with Jesus, see Chapter 14 in the Daily Prayer Guide.

Endnotes

1. Tom Ascol, "All to the Glory of God," http://www.geocities.com/Athens/Delphi/8449/passion2.html, (accessed January 2007).

2. Louie Giglio, *The Air I Breathe* (Colorado Springs, CO: Multnomah Publishers, 2003), 29.

3. Dr. John Piper, "Ambushing Satan With Song," http://www. surfinthespirit.com/music/ambushing.html (accessed January 2007).

4. *Martin Luther*, A Simple Way to Pray (Louisville, KY: Westminster Knox Press, 2000), 29.

I will…give them
joy in my house
of prayer…
for my house
will be called a
house of prayer
for all nations.
Isaiah 56:7

*To pray is to change. Prayer is
the central avenue God uses
to transform us. If we are unwilling
to change, we will abandon prayer
as a noticeable characteristic of our
lives. The more we pray, the more
we come to the heartbeat of God.
Prayer starts the communication
process between ourselves and God.
All the options of life fall before us.
At that point we will either forsake
our prayer life and cease to grow,
or we will pursue our prayer
life and let Him change us.*

—Richard Foster

CHAPTER 15

Building Your Personal House of Prayer

LET'S GET STARTED

In each room's visit in our courtyard house, we have realized that we are not alone. We are part of a family—God's family—where we can freely worship our Father as we declare His Kingdom here on earth as it is in Heaven. We have discovered that we must daily surrender our lives to Him, confess our sins, and find freedom, and He will meet our needs. As we rely on the Holy Spirit, we see His power evident in our lives.

By now, we realize that building our prayer life is about relationship, never about rules. What often trips us up is that as soon as we say we must spend an hour or two hours with God each day and walk through twelve rooms, we are setting up guidelines for ourselves that may set us up to fail. James Houston, in his book *The Transforming Power of Prayer*, says it like this:

> I used to think that prayer was a spiritual exercise— something that needed to be worked at, like running or vaulting. But I was never any good at sports, and perhaps I would never be any good at prayer either. After years of feeling useless and guilty, I began to realize the truth of a comment made by one of the early Fathers of the church, Clement of Alexandria. He said that "prayer is keeping company with God." This began to give me a new focus on prayer. I began to see prayer more as a friendship than a rigorous discipline. It started to become more of a relationship and less of a performance.[1]

So, building a house of prayer through praying the Lord's Prayer should not come across as a legalistic approach to prayer; it is simply a guideline from our Master's school of prayer. Praying is about our friendship with God.

Praying through the twelve rooms helps maintain a well-rounded prayer life. Over time, your prayer life will be more fully developed if you spend time in many of the rooms, not just a few favorite rooms. Unquestionably, follow the Holy Spirit's direction each day. Some days, you may pray in all of the rooms, and other days you may spend time in only some of the rooms. For example, depending on what you are going through in your life, you may spend a longer period of time in the declaration room, declaring what God's word says by faith.

Another time, you may focus on the warfare room, where you exercise your spiritual authority to bind demonic forces. You may spend a lot of time praying in the family room for a period of time because you need to experience your Father's love and care.

If you pray in each room for two and a half minutes, you have prayed 30 minutes. If you pray five minutes in each room, you have prayed one hour!

LISTEN FOR HIS VOICE

Learn to listen in each room. He wants to talk to you! In my book *Hearing God 30 Different Ways*,[2] I mention that we cannot limit God and how He will speak to us. He may surprise us.

It would be easy if we could just dial a number on a spiritual cell phone and hear the reassuring voice of God answering, "Hello, this is God speaking!" Yet, in reality, He is speaking to us every day in ways we often miss. The Bible says, "For God does speak—now one way, now another—though man may not perceive it" (Job 33:14).

The Bible gives us many clues to hearing God's voice. We'll discover that our ears must be tuned to hear Him. The Lord has an enormous range of options for speaking to us. He may use the inner witness of the Holy Spirit, His word, prayer, circumstances, or other people. The Lord may speak to us in dreams, visions, or even by His audible voice; however, don't expect God's audible voice to be the common way He will speak! God's voice often blends into a melodic harmony to which we have to tune in.

HEARING CLEARLY

Expect the Lord to talk to you as you walk from room to room in your house of prayer. The truth is, even when we diligently seek God for an answer, we sometimes find ourselves struggling to hear. We really want to do what the Lord wants us to do. We know that we serve a living God who speaks to us, and yet we struggle with the fact that we do not hear as clearly as we would like.

Other times we think we have heard the Lord's voice and respond to it, only to find out that we were wrong. Instead of pressing in to find out why we "missed it," we hesitate to step out in faith the next time.

Frequently it may seem as if we are trying to tune in to a weak radio signal with a lot of static. Despite our trouble with hearing, God wants to speak to us even more than we desire to hear from Him. He has so many different ways to communicate with us. We cannot put Him in a box.

Although we may wish that God would send a ten foot angel dressed in white so we have no doubt it is His voice we are hearing, I believe He often teaches us through our stumbling attempts of trial and error. Even Jesus' disciples did not always recognize His voice. When Jesus joined two of His disciples on the road to Emmaus and began to talk to them, they didn't recognize Him even though they had walked with Him, talked with Him, and eaten meals with Him for the past three years (see Luke 24:13-32). Perhaps they were so immersed in the details of the dark events of the past few days that they couldn't hear clearly.

I think there is a good chance, however, that they did not see Jesus because they simply did not expect to see Jesus. He appeared to them in an unfamiliar form, at an unexpected time, and their ears remained closed.

Before we criticize these disciples, we must ask ourselves, "How often do we experience the same loss of hearing today?" Could it be that the Lord sometimes speaks to us in ways that are unfamiliar to us, and we don't recognize His voice? We lament that we can't hear Him speak, but in reality He has been speaking all along. Could it be that our understanding of hearing His voice is limited? Maybe we have preconceived ideas how God will speak or not speak to us, and they limit us in hearing from God when He speaks.

I'm convinced we should not get too selective about the method in which the Lord speaks to us. Instead, we should stay open for the Lord to speak to us any way He desires. I spend much of my time traveling throughout the world teaching the Bible. One of the things I miss most when traveling is communicating with my family. I really miss spending time with my wife, LaVerne. Because of the technologically advanced age in which we live, I can usually communicate with her regardless of where I am in the world. I don't care whether the message comes by phone, fax, email, letter, or by a note, I just want to hear from her.

God desires to build a relationship with us. One way our relationship is built is by having ongoing dialogue with Him. It is talking and listening to each other. From the very beginning of time, God desired a two-way communication between Him and mankind. Adam and Eve were tuned to God as they "…heard the sound of the Lord God as He was walking in the garden in the cool of the day…" (Gen. 3:8).

This is how God wants to relate to us today as well. It is God's desire to walk with and to communicate with His children. He yearns for you to hear His loving, distinct voice.

The more consistent we are in spending time with Jesus, the deeper our relationship will grow, and the more clearly we will hear His voice. "Then you will call upon me and come and pray to Me, and I will listen to you. You will seek Me and find Me when you seek Me with all your heart" (Jer. 29:12-13). God listens to you!

You don't have to pray like Francis of Assisi or Billy Graham. God wants you to pray like you.

He wants us to come trusting that through prayer He can change us. We come trusting that God will lead us to repentance, lead us to being open to the Spirit's voice, and lead us to love God and others more deeply.

THE HOLY SPIRIT HELPS US PRAY

Jesus knew we needed help to pray, so He sent the Holy Spirit. "You will receive power when the Holy Spirit comes on you… (Acts 1:8). The Holy Spirit helps us to pray. "The Spirit helps us in our weakness. We do not know what we ought to pray for, but the Spirit Himself intercedes for us with groans that words cannot express" (Rom. 8:26-27). As we pray each day in the Holy Spirit, we build ourselves up in faith (Jude 20).

I like to take my Bible in one hand and think of the Holy Spirit as taking my other hand as I pray. I desperately need the Holy Spirit at my side as I step into each room of prayer.

LOOKING FOR PRAYING MEN

Now a word to us guys. For some reason, women seem to be tuned in to prayer in a way that most of us guys have not yet grasped. *Pray! Magazine* claims that 70 percent of their subscribers are women and only 30 percent are men. Something is off kilter, and needs to change. God has called men to pray. We don't have to be monks in monasteries praying for three to four hours a day to be men of prayer. It just means we are men who are willing to open our hearts to Jesus and spend time in His presence in prayer. It means we let Him transform us into His image and likeness.

Thank God for all of the millions of godly women who pray, but the Lord wants us, as men, to do our part. Let's make a commitment to the Lord today to become the men of prayer our God has called us to be. I challenge you to begin to follow the Master's plan and build a personal house of prayer today.

JESUS NEEDED A TOUCH FROM GOD EVERY DAY

Even though He was the Son of God, Jesus knew the importance of prayer. Jesus prayed before His ministry began, before a major decision, and before He started each day. He prayed during acts of healing, times of sorrow, and in the midst of temptation. Jesus prayed after a stressful day, after a victory, and after completing a job that God had given Him to do. If Jesus needed to pray every day, can we afford to do less? Imagine how exhausted Jesus must have been when He finally lay down to sleep late at night after a day of intense ministry and drifted off to sleep. Even so, Mark 1:35 says that He arose early to pray: "And in the morning, rising up a great while before day, He went out, and departed into a solitary place, and there prayed" (Mark 1:35 KJV). Jesus knew He needed to slow down from all the busyness and distractions in life and spend time in prayer. Even though Jesus led a very busy life, prayer was His focus and lifeline. He needed a touch from His Father daily.

I believe that as Jesus prayed, He gained a clearer sense of who He was (His identity) and what He was to do (His mission). The same will happen with us. Praying clarifies our very identity and mission in life.

FIND A PRAYER SPOT

I challenge you to make an agreement with the Lord to meet Him every day at the place of prayer. Not out of legalism, but out of love and obedience. Then schedule it! Here's some excellent advice from Ron Parrish in his book *From Duty to Delight*:

Finding Greater Joy in Daily Prayer:

Find out when in your day is the best time for you to connect with God. For most of us that time is when we first get out of bed. You may say: "I'm just not a morning person." If some other time works better for you, go for it. A friend of mine takes his lunch hour to seek the

Lord. Another friend sets aside time after the kids are in bed. Here's my observation: If you don't schedule it, it won't happen. It is like seeing a friend and you say, "Let's have lunch some time," and it never happens. You could be saying that same intention for the next ten years. Until we pull out our palm pilots or day-planner and set a date, it won't happen.[3]

If you choose an early morning hour, set your alarm clock. Nancy Reagan had a simple anti-drug slogan: "Just say no." The idea is that at the heart of any successful program to stop anything must be the simple will to say "no." The same is true about *starting* something. When your alarm clock starts ringing, you say "no" to sleep and make a choice to say "yes" to prayer.

I set my alarm clock on my dresser several yards away from my bed which forces me to crawl out of bed and turn it off. Although my spirit is willing and really wants to pray, my flesh is weak. These few steps early each morning between my bed and my dresser give me time needed for my body to catch up with my spirit.

I've read that some of John Wesley's early Methodist leaders who were determined to overcome the problem of drowsiness when they started praying actually soaked towels in cold water, wrapped them around their heads and went right on praying. Maybe some of us could benefit from taking a cold shower in the morning so we fully wake up for prayer.

I recommend walking. I often pace back and forth across a room or through the neighborhood if the weather permits. Some people pray in a garden or in a park. Praying as you walk can be a combination of good spiritual and physical exercise! Some people are not as sensitive to their environment, and they can pray anywhere—in a bathroom, in a hallway, in a small closet.

If your thoughts tend to wander and you have difficulty concentrating, why not pray aloud instead of silently? Spontaneous, verbal prayer allows you to hear what you are saying and keeps your thoughts focused.

Regardless of what time of day it is, it is important that you have a set *time* and *place* to pray. Jesus taught His disciples to pray by instructing them to go to a particular place: "When you pray, go into your room, close the door and pray to your Father, who is unseen. Then your Father, who sees what is done in secret, will reward you" (Matt. 6:6). Having a specific place to pray each day where you can be undisturbed is your best option.

DEVELOP YOUR PRAYER STRATEGY

The beauty of praying through twelve rooms of prayer is its framework that takes you through a sort of "physical fitness regimen" that allows for flexibility and spontaneity as you develop it. As you enter the different rooms, you know just where you are in your routine, and you can see its progression and improvement each day as you become stronger in prayer. You can develop your own emphasis and style according to what you need that day.

Obviously, you should not treat your prayer time like making a resolution to lose weight or exercise. We've all made those resolutions and failed so many times. And we will fail sometimes in prayer; however, God will help us to pray. God places within us the desire to talk with Him. His Spirit within us awakens the longing to connect with Him.

Do not get discouraged if it takes a season of time to build this prayer pattern into your life. I grew up a slow learner. All of my friends knew how to ride their bicycles, but I had the hardest time learning to keep my balance. It was embarrassing! Finally, after much perseverance, I learned to ride and could speed away with my friends. Charles Spurgeon, the famous pastor and preacher from London once said, "Through much perseverance the snail finally reached the ark." Sometimes the greatest act of spiritual warfare is to not quit!

Recently, after speaking at a church on the topic of "Building a Personal House of Prayer" emphasizing the spiritual principles contained in this book, I received this email from Wayne, a young man excited about the possibilities of using my courtyard house model and the Lord's Prayer to improve his prayer life.

> I made a quick sketch of the courtyard house you showed. The next day I went home and drew the same thing on a 2 by 3 foot sketch pad. After I was done, I started praying the Lord's Prayer according to each room of the house. The very first day of praying and using this model, I prayed an additional 30-40 minutes more than I usually do! It is awesome praying like this. I was at a place and time in my life where this was perfect for me to start doing. I just wanted to say "thank you." It is already changing my prayer and devotional time with God, and I believe the best is yet to come!

Do you want to spend time alone with someone who loves you? Your heavenly Father loves when you come to Him. Trust the Holy Spirit to lead you into deeper and more intimate times of prayer with Him. Enter the courtyard each day and discover the many facets of prayer as you experience the joy of being in the presence of God and developing a friendship with Him. And you will experience the Master's plan and become the house of prayer He has called you to be.

BUILDING YOUR PERSONAL HOUSE OF PRAYER
Apply what you've learned:

1. How would you rate your friendship with God? What do you need to do to improve it?

2. Describe different ways the Lord has spoken to you in the past.

3. Why do you think it is important to develop a prayer strategy?

4. Have you found a prayer spot? Explain.

Endnotes

1. James Houston, *The Transforming Power of Prayer* (Colorado Springs, CO: Navpress).

2. Larry Kreider, *Hearing God 30 Different Ways* (Lititz, PA: House to House Publications, 2005).

3. Ron Parrish, *From Duty to Delight: Finding Greater Joy in Daily Prayer* (Lititz, PA: Partnership Publications, 2006), 26-27.

I will...give them
joy in my house
of prayer...
for my house
will be called a
house of prayer
for all nations.
Isaiah 56:7

History is silent about revivals
that did not begin with prayer.

—Edwin Orr

Revive Us Again!

REVIVALS ARE BIRTHED IN PRAYER

I was born an American. In times past, Christian values were part of the American social and political fabric. Not so anymore. Today's society is often hostile to Christian values. The percentage of Bible-based believers has significantly decreased in America, according to recent statistics:

Builders (born 1927-1945): 65% Bible-based believers
Boomers (born 1946-1964): 35% Bible-based believers
Busters (born 1965-1983): 16% Bible-based believers
Bridgers (or Millennials, born 1984 or later):
    4% Bible-based believers

For as long as many of us can remember, we have known that when the Boomers hit a certain age, their sheer numbers would affect all of American society more than any other generation in modern times....With only 35 percent firmly believing in Scripture, they have shaped our culture with the following results: Morally corrupt films and television programs, an increasingly perverted music industry, the pornographic invasion of the Internet, civil initiatives promoting gay marriage, battles to remove the Ten Commandments from public buildings, and fights to take "under God" out of our Pledge of Allegiance....Can you imagine what America will be like when today's teens become the next generation to dominate the population, with only 4 percent currently claiming to be Bible-believing Christians?[1]

Our nation, the United States of America, is in a desperate need of revival. As I travel from continent to continent, I hear the same heart cry from believers in Christ whom I meet: "Lord, send a revival."

PREPARING FOR RAIN

What is a revival, and what causes a revival to take place?

Psalms 85:6 states, "Will you not revive us again, that your people may rejoice in You?" and Hosea 10:12 tells us, "Break up your unplowed ground; for it is time to seek the Lord, until He comes and showers righteousness on you."

Unplowed ground refers to the hardness that comes into our hearts of which we may not even be aware. It keeps us from experiencing God and true revival. Only when our hearts are softened through prayer, repentance, and faith can the Holy Spirit send His rain into our lives to refresh and revive us.

I grew up a Pennsylvania farm boy. Whenever we had times of drought on the farm, my dad and every other farmer knew that only rain would pull us through. And when we sensed the rain was finally coming, you could smell it in the air. But the soil had to be properly plowed and tilled, or the rain would erode the topsoil and the crops would be lost.

A true revival, in its most simplistic sense, is a return of obedience to God after a time of apathy or spiritual dryness. Charles Finney, who spearheaded revival in America in the early 1800s and led more than a million people to Christ, defined revival as "the Christian's new beginning of obedience to God."

According to Webster's Revised Unabridged Dictionary (1913), revival is a "renewed interest in religion, after indifference and decline; a period of religious awakening; special religious interest." When a revival comes to a person or city or region or nation, there is an awakening of people's spirits to the Spirit of God. God comes in a powerful way to change lives, families, churches, and transform communities. God actually visits an area with His presence and power, and believers become very sensitive to obey the Lord in every area of their lives.

All revivals seem to have one thing in common: they are preceded, sustained, and earmarked by a new level of prayer among God's people. Let's look at a few examples of revival from history.

THE GREAT AWAKENING

During the Reformation in Europe, God used Martin Luther, John Calvin, and others to bring spiritual change to Europe. However, by the eighteenth century there was again great spiritual darkness, and life was deeply crippled by spiritual decay and moral bankruptcy.

> In England...religion was emptied of its spirituality and power. Viewed with contempt, it became at most a code of ethics. The masses were largely untouched by the church. There were godly, faithful ministers here and there, but many clergy were mere figureheads who did not teach and actually opposed the doctrine of salvation by faith.[2]

The deplorable spiritual and social conditions set the stage for the revival efforts of John Wesley and George Whitefield. This great revival, called "The Great Awakening," could be considered the first sweeping revival to take place since the time of the apostles. While confined geographically to Great Britain and colonial America, the effect of this awakening would eventually bring radical changes to the world.

In 1739, John and Charles Wesley, George Whitefield, and about 60 others, many students from Oxford University, held a love-feast in London. Prayer continued until three in the morning, and they reported, "The power of God came mightily upon us, insomuch that many cried out for exceeding joy, and many fell to the ground (overcome by the power of God)."[3] They believed that God was about to break through in revival and spent whole nights in prayer.

Whitefield preached with great power. He was only 22 years old, but wherever he spoke, crowds flocked to hear him. His rooms were filled with praying Oxford students. Crowds increased each day at one church building until they overflowed outside and eventually twenty-thousand people gathered. God's Spirit gripped many as Whitefield preached, as did the audiences of Charles and John Wesley.

In colonial America, Jonathan Edwards, a Massachusetts pastor, began to pray for the unconverted. According to Edwards "the worst persons in the town seemed to be suddenly seized with a great degree of concern about their souls."[4] Church records of this time period indicate that as much as one-third of the population of the American colonies had had a salvation experience.

Francis Asbury is regarded as the moving force behind American Methodism. He was born in England, and at age 16 began to preach, speaking up to five times per week, walking several miles to get to each appointment. Meanwhile, help was needed desperately in America. So in 1771, when John Wesley challenged, "Who will go?" 26-year-old Asbury stepped forward. He spent the rest of his life in America and promoted the circuit rider system in America, personally traveling more than 100,000 miles to spread the Gospel, and enduring many hardships. At the time of his death in 1816, Methodism in America had grown from 5,000 members in 1776 to 214,000.

FINNEY AND THE POWER OF PRAYER

The figure who dominated America's revivalism was former lawyer Charles G. Finney. Finney's early ministry took place in western New York State. His preaching sometimes resulted in entire towns being converted. The focus of Finney's revivalism centered on social reform. He attacked every vice known to society. The roots of virtually every social reform movement of the 1800s can be traced to Finney's revival meetings. Prayer was always at the heart of the revival.

During one revival in the Rochester, New York area, Finney urged the people to pray to God earnestly and expectantly for "the immediate outpouring of His Holy Spirit." Finney wrote:

Indeed the town was full of prayer. Go where you would, you heard the voice of prayer. Pass along the streets, and if two or three Christians happened to be together they were praying. Wherever they met they prayed. Wherever there was a sinner unconverted, especially if he manifested any opposition, you would find some two or three brothers or sisters agreeing to make him a particular subject of prayer; and it was remarkable to see to what an extent God would answer prayer immediately...No one could come into the village without feeling awestricken with the impression that God was there in a peculiar and wonderful way.[5]

An eyewitness to the revivals wrote that "preaching and praying were his [Finney's] only weapons. He surrounded himself with an atmosphere of prayer, and a body of devoted praying and working Christians male and female such as New York had never before seen, and probably never since."

In September 1857, a man of prayer, Jeremiah Lanphier, started a businessmen's prayer meeting in Manhattan. By March of 1858, every church and public hall in downtown New York was filled with praying businessmen. A famous editor sent a reporter with a horse and buggy racing around to the prayer meetings to see how many men were praying. In one hour he got to only twelve meetings, but he counted 6,100 men attending. A landslide of prayer began, which overflowed to the churches in the evenings. People began to be converted, ten thousand a week in New York City alone. The movement spread throughout New England.

THE 1859 PRAYER REVIVAL IN WALES

Wales experienced revival several times throughout its history. During the second half of the nineteenth century many Welsh Christians felt the need for a spiritual awakening. They prayed privately and in churches, asking God for revival. God used a twenty-six-year-old Methodist, Rev. Humphrey Jones and another pastor, David Morgan, who worked together in ministry to influence this revival.

Beginning at 5:00 A.M. every day, even in the busiest days of harvest…people lined the roads for a half mile in all directions. Young and old came and, in a very orderly way, prayed, praised, and worshiped. Prayer meetings were held each night….The revival fire and blessings spread from church to church among all denominations, into outlying villages and other counties. A tremendous work of God spread through the men working in the huge state quarries. Revival spread like a belt of fire encircling the mountains.[6]

HARVEST IN AMERICA

The revival in Wales was of great interest to the Christians and Christian press in America. The New York Herald gave extensive coverage to the prayer meeting revival. Not to be outdone, the New York Tribune devoted an entire issue in April 1858 to news of the revival. News of the revival quickly traveled westward by telegraph. This was the first revival in which the media played an important role in spreading the revival.

Revival blessings and conversions were reported in towns and cities across the state. Within four months, the Methodists alone reported ten thousand conversions in Philadelphia. Revival spread quickly from Pennsylvania to New Jersey. In Atlantic City, not more than 50 unconverted people were reported to be remaining in a population of sixty thousand. In Schenectady, New York, all evangelical denominations joined in prayer in evangelistic rallies, and the revival movement continued for months.

About a thousand businessmen met in Atlanta to pray for an outpouring of the Holy Spirit. On November 2, in an unprecedented way, stores, factories, and offices closed at noon for prayer. The Supreme Court and even saloons closed so people could attend prayer meetings. In simultaneous meetings in Louisville, Kentucky, there were fifteen hundred inquirers, and one thousand joined the churches at once. Soon the press reported "the most remarkable revival ever known," with four thousand recorded conversions in the city. Fifty-eight leading business firms closed at noon for prayer meetings. In Danville, Kentucky, all businesses closed, and management and employees attended services as a body. In Paducah, Kentucky, Southern Baptists reported that God sent "a great Pentecostal revival" that lasted for five months. One church alone added one thousand new members.[7]

CONTINUED REVIVAL IN WALES

The Welsh Church continued praying fervently, and by 1902, 2,000 prayer groups had formed all over Wales. In 1904, a series of mighty revivals began. The Holy Spirit anointed a 25-year-old unknown Welsh coal miner by the name of Evan Roberts who was instrumental in this move of God.

For thirteen years Evan Roberts had prayed for a move of God's Spirit. Every time the church doors were open, this young man was there on the front pew. One year prior to the revival that flooded Wales, the Spirit of God broke through and washed over this young man. He prayed so loud and so hard that his landlady kicked him out of his apartment. Here was his prayer: *Bend me. Bend me. Bend me, O Lord.*

Because Evan Roberts prayed, fasted, and sought God, he had a vision in 1904 that the revival would see a hundred thousand people saved in Wales and would literally sweep around the world. He was loudly ridiculed and scorned by religious leaders; nevertheless, within five months, the revival added a hundred thousand people to the Church.[8]

The revival moved through central Europe, Norway, and Scandinavia. It spread down to Africa and India, through China and into Korea. Healings, visions, signs, and wonders such as those recorded in the book of Acts were witnessed throughout the revival in the early 1900s. The Church added more than a million people to its rolls and at least that many more were reportedly saved.

REVIVAL PRAYER TODAY

A few weeks before I wrote this chapter, I joined thousands of Korean youth in a stadium in Seoul Korea who were praying all night for another visitation of the Lord's Spirit like the revival of one hundred years ago that spread from Wales to India to Korea. Lord, send rain in our generation!

This week I was worshiping with more than forty thousand believers from 65 nations in Sydney, Australia, crying out to God for revival. Lord, revive us again! And today, as I write these words from a hotel in Australia, more than 60,000 believers, including both young and old, are gathered together in Nashville, Tennessee, at "The Call" with one purpose: to cry out to God for revival among the youth of the United States of America. *Lord, send rain!*

PRAY FOR THE HARVEST!

Great moves of God are always preceded by prayer and obedience. In Acts 2:41 we read that the Lord added three thousand to the church. As the early believers kept praying, multitudes were added to the early church (see Acts 5:1). The early church was a praying church and experienced exponential growth. Tommy Barnett says this about the connection between prayer and the harvest of souls:

> If we really believed that prayer changes things, then every day we would pray for our children, for our nation and for new converts. We have not seen a harvest or workers for the harvest because we have not prayed and asked God. We act as though prayer is not really important and as though we have matured beyond the need to pray. In all of history, the church has never been so organized, computerized, specialized, and equipped with surveys, data and statistics. Yes, all of these sources of information are wonderful, but if we are not careful, we will begin neglecting prayer and looking to our organization for power. Only prayer will loose the chains of bondage and release the power of the Gospel to a hurting world.[9]

We must pray and ask the Holy Spirit to show us anything in our lives (including prayerlessness) that could hinder us from experiencing true revival. Next to the Bible, the book that has shaped my life more than any other is *Revival Lectures* by Charles Finney. He said that revival was not a miracle, but it is the result of the right use of the appropriate means:

> It is impossible for us to say that there is not as direct an influence or agency from God, to produce a crop of grain, as there is to produce a revival....In the Bible, the word of God is compared to grain, and preaching is compared to sowing seed, and the results to the springing up and growth of the crop....I wish this idea to be impressed on all your minds, for there has long been an idea prevalent...that there is no connection of the means with the result, and no tendency in the means to produce the effect. No doctrine is more dangerous than this to the prosperity of the church, and nothing more absurd. Suppose a man were to go and preach...among farmers, about their sowing grain. Let him tell them that God is a sovereign, and will give them a crop only when it pleases him, and that for them to plow and plant and labor as if they expected to raise a crop is very wrong, and taking the work out of the hands of God, that it interferes with His sovereignty, and is going on in their own strength; and that there is no connection between the means and the result on which they can depend. And now, suppose the farmers should believe such doctrine. Why, they would starve the world to death....The connection is as clear in religion as it is when the farmer sows his grain.[10]

When our hearts long for God more than anything else, then we move into the realm of prayer that brings us to the very throne room of God. God hears the passionate prayers of His people. As we intercede before God for people without Christ, His Spirit will make it happen. "Not by might, nor by power, but by My Spirit, says the Lord" is the very foundation for revival.

I HAVE A DREAM

I have a dream. This is a dream that I share with millions of God's people in the nations of the world—that our God would visit His people in our generation, both young and old together, in a way that we will experience His power and presence in our families, our churches, our communities and our nations like never before. Acts 2:17-18 declares it so boldly and so clearly: "In the last days, God says, I will [*not might*] pour out My Spirit on all people. Your sons and daughters will [*not might*] prophesy, your young men will [*not might*] see visions, your old men will [*not might*] dream dreams. Even on My servants, both men and women, I will [*not might*] pour out My Spirit in those days, and they will [*not might*] prophesy" [*italics my addition*].

This Scripture was fulfilled at Pentecost—yet God desires an even greater fulfillment as thousands more turn to Him and receive the outpouring of His Holy Spirit. He is simply asking us to pray. Remember the words of John Wesley, "God does everything by prayer and nothing without it."

Lord, revive us again. Continue to teach us to pray.

REVIVE US AGAIN!
Apply what you've learned:

1. Describe in your own words what a revival is.

2. Do you agree that America is in need of revival? Discuss.

3. Pray for the Holy Spirit to show those things in your life (including prayerlessness) that could hinder you from experiencing revival.

4. In light of our nation needing revival, what is God saying to me personally to prepare for it?

ENDNOTES

1. Ron Luce, *Battle Cry for a Generation* (Colorado Springs, CO: NexGen, 2005), 30-31.

2. Wesley Duewel, *Revial Fire* (Grand Rapids, MI: Zondervan Publishing House, 1995), 50.

3. Ibid., 53.

4. Jeff Ziegler and Jay Rogers, "Revival and Spiritual Awakening," http://forerunner.com/forerunner/X0606_Revival_Spiritual_A.html, (accessed January 2008).

5. Duewel, Revival Fire, 101

6. Ibid., 161.

7. Ibid., 209-210.

8. Tommy Barnett, *Multiplication* (Orlando, FL: Creation House, 1997), 82.

9. Ibid., 129.

10. Charles G. Finney, *Revival Lectures* (Tarrytown, NY: Fleming H. Revell Company), 5.

12 Rooms in
Your Personal House of Prayer

Provision Room
Give us today our daily bread

Forgiveness Room
Forgive us our debts

Freedom Room
As we also have forgiven our debtors

Protection Room
And lead us not into temptation

Surrender Room
Your will be done, on earth as it is in Heaven

Warfare Room
But deliver us from the evil one

I will…give them joy in my house of prayer… for my house will be called a house of prayer for all nations.
Isaiah 56:7

Declaration Room
Your kingdom come

Kingdom Room
For Yours is the kingdom

Adoration Room
Hallowed be Your name

Family Room
Our Father in Heaven

Exaltation Room
And the glory forever. Amen.

Power Room
And the power

Daily Prayer Guide

This Prayer Guide is designed to be used every day as you meet with the Lord in prayer. Use it to share your heart and move toward an ever increasing intimate friendship with Jesus. It's designed with prayers and Scriptures to pray as you progress through each part of the Lord's Prayer, and has room to add additional Scriptures and prayer concerns.

Along with this Guide, I encourage you to daily keep a prayer journal and jot down some of the things that you pray for—your own prayer concerns, prayer for others, Scriptures that speak to you, impressions the Lord gives to you, and answers to prayer. One of the greatest encouragements in daily prayer is answered prayer. Use your prayer journal as a record to help you observe and thank God for the way that He answers your prayers.

THE FAMILY ROOM

CHAPTER 3

Our Father in Heaven (Matthew 6:9).

Thank You, Lord, that I can have personal and direct access to You. You are never too busy for me.

...call upon Me and come and pray to Me, and I will listen to you (Jeremiah 29:12).

I'm grateful that I can meet You in the family room and know Your love—You are my Father. Thank You Lord, I know that You totally love and accept me today because I am Your child.

How great is the love the Father has lavished on us, that we should be called children of God! (1 John 3:1)

I know that I am loved by You as my heavenly Daddy, because the Bible tells me so. Lord, I believe in You.

For God so loved the world that He gave His one and only Son, that whoever believes in Him shall not perish but have eternal life. (John 3:16)

I can relax and rest in You, because I am at home in Your house.

Come with Me by yourselves to a quiet place and get some rest (Mark 6:31).

Despite what I am feeling today, You love me and will not reject me. You are with me and will help me and give me strength today. I will not fear.

I have chosen you and have not cast you away: Fear not, for I am with you; Be not be dismayed, for I am your God. I will strengthen you, Yes, I will help you, I will uphold you with My righteous right hand...For I, the Lord your God, will hold your right hand, Saying to you, "Fear not, I will help you" (Isaiah 41:9b,10,13 NKJV).

You know my needs, cares, temptations, and problems today. I come boldly to You in my time of need.

Let us then approach the throne of grace with confidence, so that we may receive mercy and find grace to help us in our time of need (Hebrews 4:16).

Lord, Your word is filled with power.

For the word of God is living and active. Sharper than any double-edged sword, it penetrates even to dividing soul and spirit, joints and marrow; it judges the thoughts and attitudes of the heart (Hebrews 4:12-13).

Thank You for transforming me by Your love, so I can freely serve others.

As the Father loved Me, I also have loved you... (John 15:9 NKJV).

...Serve one another in love (Galatians 5:13).

Pray with an open Bible. Fill your prayers with God's word. Meditate on it.

Add additional Scriptures to meditate on and prayers to pray below.

_____

_____

_____

_____

Take a few minutes to be still before the Lord. He is your Father, You are His child. Observe if He gives You any more impressions of His love for you. Write them down in your journal along with any other prayer requests or answers to prayer.

THE ADORATION ROOM

CHAPTER 4

Hallowed be Your Name (Matthew 6:9).

Lord, Your name is holy. Here in the adoration room, I bless Your holy name.

> *Who among the gods is like You, O Lord? Who is like You—majestic in holiness...* (Exodus 15:11).

> *Holy, holy, holy, is the Lord of hosts...* (Isaiah 6:3 NKJV).

> *Praise His holy name* (Psalm 103:1).

Jesus, I exalt Your name as above all other names—the most powerful name in Heaven and earth.

> *Therefore God exalted Him to the highest place and gave Him the name that is above every name, that at the name of Jesus every knee should bow...and every tongue confess that Jesus Christ is Lord, to the glory of God the Father* (Philippians 2:9-11).

I refuse to be controlled by my feelings or circumstances today. I am righteous through faith in Jesus Christ.

> *Those who receive God's abundant provision of grace and of the gift of righteousness reign in life through the one man, Jesus Christ* (Romans 5:17).

Speak the names of God that answer your specific need right now. For example: Jesus, You are my...Father, great King, Provider (see Gen. 22:14), Peace (see Judg. 6:24), Counselor, Sufficiency, Righteousness (see Jer. 23:6; 33:16), Healer (see Exod. 15:26; Jer. 30:17, 3:22; Isaiah 61:1), Sanctifier (see Exod. 31:13; Lev. 20:7-8), Shepherd (see Ps. 23:1,4,6; 1 Cor. 15:55-57), Maker, Comfort,

Strength, Salvation, wise God, Shield, Deliverer, Banner (see Exod. 17:15).

Lord, thank You that You are Wonderful, Counselor, The Mighty God, The Everlasting Father, and the Prince of Peace

And His name shall be called Wonderful, Counselor, The mighty God, The everlasting Father, The Prince of Peace (Isaiah 9:6 KJV).

Our Father in Heaven, You are:

The Lord our Provider, Jehovah-Jireh (see Gen. 22:14).

The Lord our Banner, Jehovah-Nissi (see Exod. 17:15).

The Lord our Peace, Jehovahi-Shalom (see Judg. 6:24).

The Lord who is Present, Jehovah—Shammah (see Ezek. 48:35).

The Lord of Hosts, Jehovah-Tsebaoth (see 1 Sam. 1:3; Isa. 48:2).

The Lord God of Israel, Jehovah-Elohe Israel (see Isa. 1:24).

The Lord our Righteousness, Jehovah-Tsidkenu (see Jer. 23:6; 33:16).

The Lord our Healer (body, soul, and spirit), Jehovah-Rophe (see Exod. 15:26; Jer. 30:17, 3:22; Isa. 61:1).

The Lord our Sanctifier, Jehovah-M'kaddesh (see Exod. 31:13; Lev. 20:7-8).

The Lord our Shepherd, Jehovah-Rohi (see John 10:11; Heb. 13:20).

The Lord our Maker, Jehovah-Hoseenu (see Ps. 95:6).

You are in a class by yourself, Lord—awesome and great, the Creator of the entire universe, completely opposite from what I am.

For My thoughts are not your thoughts, nor are your ways My ways, says the Lord. For as the heavens are higher than the earth, so are My ways higher than your ways, and My thoughts than your thoughts (Isaiah 55:8-9 NKJV).

Lord, even though You are a holy God, You yearn for a relationship with me. That is why I pray every day. I want to know You better.

Now this is eternal life: that they may know You, the only true God, and Jesus Christ, whom You have sent (John 17:3).

Lord, today's encounter with You changes me, those I pray for, and those I meet today in an ever-increasing way.

And we, who with unveiled faces all reflect the Lord's glory, are being transformed into His likeness with ever-increasing glory, which comes from the Lord, who is the Spirit (2 Corinthians 3:18).

Add additional Scriptures to meditate on and prayers to pray below.

_____

_____

_____

_____

Take a few minutes to be still before the Lord. He is your King; you are His friend. Observe if He gives you any more impressions of who He is in your life. Write them down in your journal along with any other prayer requests or answers to prayer. Tell God you love Him and adore Him in the adoration room. Reflect on His greatness (see Ps. 8:1-9).

THE DECLARATION ROOM

CHAPTER 5

Your Kingdom come (Matthew 6:10).

Lord, You have invited me into Your Kingdom, and You are active here on earth just as You are in Heaven.

> *The Kingdom of the world has become the Kingdom of our Lord and of His Christ, and He will reign for ever and ever* (Revelation 11:15).

Here in the declaration room, I thank You for the new Kingdom You set up in my heart when I was born again.

> *I tell you the truth, no one can see the Kingdom of God unless He is born again* (John 3:3).

I declare that Your Kingdom comes as I submit my life to You. Change me from the inside out.

> *And we, who with unveiled faces all reflect the Lord's glory, are being transformed into His likeness with ever-increasing glory, which comes from the Lord, who is the Spirit* (2 Corinthians 3:18).

I declare today, "As for me and my household, we will serve the Lord" (Josh. 24:15).

I declare with Jesus, "He will build His Church, and the gates of hell will not prevail against it!" (see Matt. 16:18).

I declare, "I am not ashamed of the Gospel of Christ: for it is the power of God unto salvation!" (Rom. 1:16 KJV).

I declare that, "Greater is He that is in me than He who is in the world" (see 1 John 4:4 KJV).

I declare, "I have been crucified with Christ and I no longer live, but Christ lives in me. The life I live in the body, I live by faith in the Son of God, who loved me and gave Himself for me" (Galatians 2:20).

Lord, I submit to You and resist the devil in Your name.

Submit yourselves, then, to God. Resist the devil, and he will flee from you (James 4:7).

I stand in the victory that You have won for me and choose to walk in righteousness, peace, and joy.

For the Kingdom of God is not a matter of eating and drinking, but of righteousness, peace, and joy in the Holy Spirit (Romans 14:17).

I declare Your Word over myself, my family, church, my community, my nation, circumstances, my finances.

Lord, help me to see how we all need to change to be more what You want.

For the word of God is living and active (Hebrews 4:12).

The prayer of a righteous man is powerful and effective (James 5:16).

I pray for my family members, neighbors, and others the Lord has placed in my life to pray for.

I pray that out of His glorious riches He may strengthen you with power through His Spirit in your inner being, so that Christ may dwell in your hearts through faith. And I pray that you, being rooted and established in love, may have power, together with all the saints, to grasp how wide and long and high and deep is the love of Christ, and to know this love that surpasses knowledge-that you may be filled to the measure of all the fullness of God. Now to Him who is able to do immeasurably more than all we ask or imagine, according to His power that is at work within us, to Him be glory in the Church and in Christ Jesus throughout all generations, for ever and ever! Amen (Ephesians 3:16-21).

I pray for my church _____ and for my spiritual
leaders _____ that they would be filled with wisdom and spiritual understanding.

I pray for the president _____ and other government officials _____ that they would seek God for
wisdom so they are effective in office.

I pray for missionaries _____ to clearly communicate the Gospel to those they want to reach.

Pray for their personal needs: health, safety, victory over dis-
couragement, and loneliness.

Declare "who you are in Christ."

(For a complete list, see Appendix A.)

I am now God's child. (See First John 3:2.)

I am born of the imperishable seed of God's Word. (See First
Peter 1:23.)

I am loved by Christ and freed from my sins. (See Revelation
1:5.)

I am forgiven all my sins. (See Ephesians 1:7.)

I am justified from all things. (See Acts 13:39.)

I am the righteousness of God. (See Second Corinthians
5:21.)

I am free from all condemnation. (See Romans 8:1.)

I can forget the past. (See Philippians 3:13.)

I am a new creature. (See Second Corinthians 5:17.)

I am the temple of the Holy Spirit. (See First Corinthians
6:19.)

I am redeemed from the curse of the law. (See Galatians
3:13.)

I am reconciled to God. (See Second Corinthians 5:18.)

I am beloved of God. (See First John 4:10.)

I am a saint and loved by God. (See Romans 1:7.)

I am holy and without blame before Him. (See Ephesians
1:4.)

I am the head and not the tail. (See Deuteronomy 28:13.)

I am called of God by the grace given in Christ. (See First
Timothy 1:9.)

I am brought near by the blood of Christ. (See Ephesians
2:13.)

I have been given fullness in Christ. (See Colossians 2:10.)

Add additional Scriptures to meditate on and prayers to pray
below.

_____

_____

_____

_____

Take a few minutes to be still before the Lord. He is your
God, you are His co-laborer. Observe if He gives you any more
impressions of areas He may be calling you to declare. Write them
down in your journal along with any other prayer requests, Scriptures, or answers to prayer.

The Surrender

Chapter 6

Your will be done, on earth as it is in Heaven (Matthew 6:10).

Lord, in the surrender room, I invite You into my life here on earth and give up everything that keeps me from wanting your ways first.

Father...not my will, but yours be done (Luke 22:42).

Lord, my very life belongs completely to You.
I choose to obey and submit to You today.
I seek first Your Kingdom (see Matt. 6:33) so that Your Kingdom comes to all people.
I pray that everyone You have placed in my life receives the benefit of living on a planet where Your will is done! This includes

_____ .

I surrender *all* to You and acknowledge You as Lord over all areas of my life.

Lean not on your own understanding; in all your ways acknowledge Him, and He will make your paths straight (Proverbs 3:5-6).

Surrendering may involve waiting. Lord, I will wait in silence, alert to what You may say to me.

My soul waits in silence for God (Psalm 62:1 NASB).

My soul waits for the Lord more than watchmen wait for the morning (Psalm 130:6).

Those who wait on the Lord shall renew their strength (Isaiah 40:31 NKJV).

Lord, I know that submission and resting go hand-in-hand. I give You my cares today. I cast them all on You.

Cast all your anxiety on Him because He cares for you (1 Peter 5:7).

Lord may I only take on burdens that You give to me, not those I give myself and those that others give to me. Your yoke is easy and Your burden is light.

Come to Me, all you who are weary and burdened, and I will give you rest. Take My yoke upon you and learn from Me, for I am gentle and humble in heart, and you will find rest for your souls. For My yoke is easy and My burden is light (Matthew 11:28-30).

Thank You Lord, that Your commandments are not burdensome.

And His commands are not burdensome (1 John 5:3).

Lord, I choose to be content today no matter what I am going through, as I surrender to You.

...for I have learned to be content whatever the circumstances (Philippians 4:11).

"Lord, I know You are in charge. I am satisfied with Your provision and goodness and what You determine as best for me now. Therefore, I am perfectly content."

All to Jesus, I surrender;
All to You I freely give;
I will ever love and trust You,
In Your presence daily live.
I surrender all, I surrender all,
All to You, my blessed Savior,
I surrender all.[1]

ENDNOTE

1. Lyrics written by Judson W. Van DeVenter, 1896.

Lord, "Come and set up Your Kingdom, so that everyone on earth will obey You, as You are obeyed in Heaven" (Matt. 6:10 CEV).

Add additional Scriptures to meditate on and prayers to pray below.

_____

_____

_____

_____

Take a few minutes to be still before the Lord. He is the King of the universe, and we are His servants. Observe if He gives you any more impressions of areas He may be calling you to surrender to Him. Write them down in your journal along with any other prayer requests, Scriptures, or answers to prayer.

THE PROVISION ROOM

CHAPTER 7

Give us today our daily bread (Matthew 6:11).

Lord, here in the provision room, I am going to ask for daily bread, abundant provision. You tell us to ask and that we do not have because we do not ask.

...You do not have because you do not ask (James 4:2 NKJV).

Lord, You tell us to, "...ask and it will be given to you; seek and you will find; knock and the door will be opened to you. For everyone who asks receives; he who seeks finds; and to him who knocks, the door will be opened" (Luke 11:9-10). I ask in faith in Jesus' name!

I depend on You to provide my daily needs like the birds and the wildflowers depend on You (see Matt 6:25-34).

I will not worry but instead thank You ahead of time for providing because I know I should "...not be anxious about anything, but in everything, by prayer and petition, with thanksgiving, present [my] requests to God" (Phil. 4:6).

Lord, You are El Shaddai, the God who is "more than enough."

Thank You for doing immeasurably more than all I could even ask or imagine today (see Eph. 3:20).

Your supply is limitless and abundant blessing is Your nature.

I will look on you with favor and make you fruitful and increase your numbers, and I will keep My covenant with you. You will still be eating last year's harvest when you will have to move it out to make room for the new (Leviticus 26:9-10).

(See also Exodus 36:3-7; Deuteronomy 7:13-14; 28:1-14; 2 Kings 4; 2 Chronicles 20; Psalm 23; Proverbs 3:9-10; Malachi 3:10-12.)

Thank You for giving me a surplus so that I have extra to give to others (see 3 John 2).

Help me to manage my resources, Lord, in a godly way.

So then, men ought to regard us as servants of Christ and as those entrusted with the secret things of God. Now it is required that those who have been given a trust must prove faithful....For who makes you different from anyone else? What do you have that you did not receive? And if you did receive it, why do you boast as though you did not? (1 Corinthians 4:1-2,7)

I choose to allow my resources to be used for Your Kingdom as I honor You with a tithe and give offerings (see Gen. 14:18-20; Prov. 3:9-10; 1 Cor. 16:2; Mal. 3:8-11).

Read Psalm 103, and its list of benefits. Pray these benefits and provisions over your life in the provision room.

Lord, You promised in Deuteronomy 28:

- If you fully obey the Lord your God and carefully follow all His commands I give you today, the Lord your God will set you high above all the nations on earth. All these blessings will come upon you and accompany you if you obey the Lord your God:
- You will be blessed in the city and blessed in the country.
- The fruit of your womb will be blessed, and the crops of your land and the young of your livestock—the calves of your herds and the lambs of your flocks.
- Your basket and your kneading trough will be blessed.
- You will be blessed when you come in and blessed when you go out.
- The Lord will grant that the enemies who rise up against you will be defeated before you. They will come at you from one direction but flee from you in seven.
- The Lord will send a blessing on your barns and on everything you put your hand to. The Lord your God will bless you in the land He is giving you.

- The Lord will establish you as His holy people, as He promised you on oath, if you keep the commands of the Lord your God and walk in His ways.
- Then all the peoples on earth will see that you are called by the name of the Lord, and they will fear you.
- The Lord will grant you abundant prosperity—in the fruit of your womb, the young of your livestock, and the crops of your ground—in the land He swore to your forefathers to give you.
- The Lord will open the heavens, the storehouse of His bounty, to send rain on your land in season and to bless all the work of your hands.
- You will lend to many nations but will borrow from none.
- The Lord will make you the head, not the tail.
- If you pay attention to the commands of the Lord your God that I give you this day and carefully follow them, you will always be at the top, never at the bottom.

I claim these promises for my life and for the lives of my loved ones in Jesus' name. I pray for _____ who is in great need of provision right now. Lord, use me as Your vessel of blessing.

List any other promises the Holy Spirit shows you that you can claim below.

_____

_____

_____

_____

Take a few minutes to be still before the Lord. He is your Father and your provider. You are His child. Observe if He gives you any more impressions of areas He may be calling you to ask Him for provision both for you and for others. Write them down in your journal along with any other prayer requests, Scriptures, or answers to prayer.

The Forgiveness Room

Chapter 8

Forgive us our debts (Matthew 6:12).

Lord, here in the forgiveness room, I want You to address three issues in my life—
1. my sin
2. Your forgiveness for my sin
3. how to access that forgiveness through confession

1. *My sin:*

I know that if I harbor sin in my life, I will have trouble communicating with You. Lord, I am in agreement with You regarding any sin in my life.

> *When I kept silent, my bones grew old Through my groaning all the day long. For day and night Your hand was heavy upon me; My vitality was turned into the drought of summer. I acknowledged my sin to You, And my iniquity I have not hidden. I said, "I will confess my transgressions to the Lord," And You forgave the iniquity of my sin* (Psalm 32:3-5 NKJV).

I do not excuse my sin because I know that sin means I have missed the bull's eye. Anything off the center of Your will is sin.

2. *Your forgiveness for my sin:*

I know You will completely forgive me of my sins (my debts). Your blood cleanses me and makes me pure before You.

> *But if we walk in the light, as He is in the light, we have fellowship with one another, and the blood of Jesus, His Son, purifies us from all sin* (1 John 1:7).

Lord, I ask for Your forgiveness, and You say, "it is remembered no more!"

> *As far as the east is from the west, so far has He removed our transgressions from us* (Psalm 103:12).

**3. *Lord, I access Your forgiveness (move from sin to forgiveness)
by confession:***
I ask for Your forgiveness right now. "Forgive my debts!" I
confess my sin (admit my guilt).

> *If I had cherished sin in my heart, the Lord would not have lis-
> tened; but God has surely listened and heard my voice in
> prayer. Praise be to God, who has not rejected my prayer or
> withheld His love from me! (Psalm 66:18-20)*

Lord, I ask You to cleanse and restore me today.
Here in the forgiveness room, I know that confessing is a daily
activity because I am not perfect.

> *If we claim to be without sin, we deceive ourselves...If we
> confess our sins, He is faithful and just and will forgive us our
> sins and purify us from all unrighteousness... (1 John 1:8-9).*

> *But if anybody does sin, we have one who speaks to the
> Father in our defense—Jesus Christ, the Righteous One...
> (1 John 2:1).*

I refuse to struggle with false guilt or condemnation.

> *If we confess our sins, He is faithful and just and will forgive
> us our sins and purify us from all unrighteousness (1 John
> 1:9).*

Take time in the forgiveness room to be still before the Lord
and ask Him to reveal anything you may have missed.
He is your Father who is eagerly waiting to forgive you. You
are His beloved child. Observe if He gives you any more impressions of areas He wants you to ask Him for forgiveness.

> *See if there is any wicked way in me, and lead me in the way
> everlasting (Psalm 139:24 NKJV).*

> *Create in me a pure heart, O God, and renew a steadfast
> spirit within me (Psalm 51:10).*

Add additional Scriptures to meditate on and prayers to pray below.

_____

_____

_____

_____

In your prayer journal list these areas you know your loving heavenly Father has forgiven you of because of His shed blood on the cross. Also, write down any other prayer requests or Scriptures He may be giving to you.

The Freedom Room

Chapter 9

As we also have forgiven our debtors (Matthew 6:12).

Lord, I realize that a key to finding freedom is forgiving others.

For if you forgive men when they sin against you, your heavenly Father will also forgive you. But if you do not forgive men their sins, your Father will not forgive your sins (Matthew 6:14-15).

Search my heart, Lord, to see if there is any unforgiveness there. I don't want a root of bitterness to grow.

See to it that no one misses the grace of God and that no bitter root grows up to cause trouble and defile many (Hebrews 12:15).

Lord, I forgive _____ (place individuals' names here) in Jesus' name. I know that what they did was wrong, but I ask You to forgive them and I pray that You will bless them. Father, forgive them, for they did not know what they were doing.

Lord, help me to become "offense proof" today.

Guard my heart so that I will not look to give offense, nor look to find offense. Restore both me and those I forgive into your fellowship, Lord. I refuse to allow the devil to accuse me to God, allow the devil to accuse God to me, allow the devil to accuse me to others, allow the devil to accuse others to me, or allow the devil to accuse me to myself!

Help me, Lord, to forgive and receive freedom from You when I am hurt by others.

Help me to rejoice in opportunities to show mercy rather than expecting strict justice.

...judgment without mercy will be shown to anyone who has not been merciful. Mercy triumphs over judgment! (James 2:13)

Lord, I trust You to set me free as I have forgiven.

Christ redeemed us from the curse of the law by becoming a curse for us...The reason the Son of God appeared was to destroy the devil's work (Galatians 3:13a; 1 John 3:8b).

I am free from the devil's lies over my life because I am free from the curse. I reclaim what satan stole from me, in Jesus' name.

Lord, I receive Your healing of the memories of what has happened in Jesus' name. I am willing to receive prayer from a trusted friend if needed.

Therefore confess your sins to each other and pray for each other so that you may be healed. The prayer of a righteous man is powerful and effective (James 5:16).

Lord, I will be patient knowing the process may not happen overnight.

My trust is in You to obtain a full recovery. "...Imitate those who through faith and patience inherit what has been promised" (Heb. 6:12b).

Lord, today I turn accusation into intercession in the freedom room, knowing that "mercy triumphs over judgment!"

...Mercy triumphs over judgment! (James 2:13).

Add additional Scriptures to meditate on and prayers to pray below.

_____

_____

_____

_____

In your journal, list areas you need freedom in. Take a few minutes to be still before the Lord. He is your heavenly Father who has forgiven you completely. You are His beloved child. Observe if He gives you any more impressions of persons He is asking you to forgive. Forgive them in Jesus' name.

Write in your journal areas you know you have found freedom in through your loving heavenly Father who has forgiven you so you can forgive others. Also, write down any other prayer requests, answers to prayer, or Scriptures He may be giving to you.

THE PROTECTION ROOM

CHAPTER 10

And lead us not into temptation (Matthew 6:13).

Lord, I depend on You to keep me from sin.
I pray for Your help and victory in this _____
(temptation) in my life.

Pray that you may not enter into temptation (Luke 22:40 NKJV).

The spirit indeed is willing, but the flesh is weak (Matthew 26:41 NKJV).

I know You understand temptations I face because You were tempted like me.

For we do not have a High Priest who cannot sympathize with our weaknesses, but was in all points tempted as we are, yet without sin... (Hebrews 4:15 NKJV).

I come boldly to You today to find mercy and grace.
I come boldly to You today to find mercy, knowing that each time of temptation and testing is an opportunity to grow and find grace.

Let us therefore come boldly to the throne of grace, that we may obtain mercy and find grace to help in time of need (Hebrews 4:16 NKJV).

Help me, Lord, not to allow wrong thoughts and actions to gain control and become sin in my life.

But each one is tempted when he is drawn away by His own desires and enticed. Then, when desire has conceived, it gives birth to sin; and sin, when it is full-grown, brings forth death (James 1:14-15 NKJV).

I know that temptation does not come from You, Lord.

When tempted, no one should say, "God is tempting me." For God cannot be tempted by evil, nor does He tempt anyone (James 1:13).

Lord, here in the protection room, I ask for Your power to keep me from yielding to temptation.

No temptation has seized you except what is common to man. And God is faithful; He will not let you be tempted beyond what you can bear...(1 Corinthians 10:13).

Blessed is the man who perseveres under trial, because when he has stood the test, he will receive the crown of life... (James 1:12).

Protect me today, Lord, from three main areas of temptation: coveting, lust, and pride.

"For everything in the world—the cravings of sinful man, the lust of His eyes and the boasting of what he has and does— comes not from the Father but from the world" (1 John 2:16).

Lord, I ask that You would grant me grace to walk in generosity, purity, and humility.

Thank You Lord, for the grace to endure temptation for Your glory.

"Blessed is the man who endures temptation; for when he has been approved, he will receive the crown of life which the Lord has promised to those who love Him" (James 1:12 NKJV).

Today, I trust You to protect my life and my loved ones from temptation and harm.

Take time to listen to the Holy Spirit as you pray through Psalm 91. Place your name and those you are praying for in the Scripture and claim each promise.

He who dwells in the shelter of the Most High
will rest in the shadow of the Almighty.
I will say of the Lord, "He is my refuge and my fortress,
my God, in whom I trust."
Surely He will save you from the fowler's snare
and from the deadly pestilence.
He will cover you with His feathers,
and under His wings you will find refuge;
His faithfulness will be your shield and rampart.
You will not fear the terror of night,
nor the arrow that flies by day,
nor the pestilence that stalks in the darkness,
nor the plague that destroys at midday.
A thousand may fall at your side,
ten thousand at your right hand,
but it will not come near you.
You will only observe with your eyes
and see the punishment of the wicked.
If you make the Most High your dwelling—
even the Lord, who is my refuge—
then no harm will befall you,
no disaster will come near your tent.
For He will command His angels concerning you
to guard you in all your ways;
they will lift you up in their hands,
so that you will not strike your foot against a stone.
You will tread upon the lion and the cobra;
you will trample the great lion and the serpent.
"Because He loves me," says the Lord, "I will rescue him;
I will protect him, for He acknowledges my name.
He will call upon Me, and I will answer him;
I will be with him in trouble,
I will deliver him and honor him.
With long life will I satisfy him
and show him My salvation" (Psalm 91).

Add additional Scriptures to meditate on and prayers to pray below.

_____

_____

_____

_____

Pray for protection for your family, spiritual leaders, leaders in government, and for missionaries. Take a few minutes to be still before the Lord. Observe if He gives you any more impressions of individuals He wants you to pray protection over. Write in your journal those times, both present and past, when you know you have experienced the Lord's protection. Also, write down any other prayer requests, answers to prayer, or Scriptures He may be giving to you.

THE WARFARE ROOM

CHAPTER 11

But deliver us from the evil one (Matthew 6:13).

Lord, the Scriptures teach us:

...though we live in the world, we do not wage war as the world does. The weapons we fight with are not the weapons of the world. On the contrary, they have divine power to demolish strongholds. We demolish arguments and every pretension that sets itself up against the knowledge of God, and we take captive every thought to make it obedient to Christ (2 Corinthians 10:3-5).

I bring every thought that I have captive to the obedience of Christ today in Jesus' name!

Lord, here in the warfare room, I am aware that I am engaged in a spiritual battle.

Satan wants me to fail, but You have guaranteed me victory. Today I choose to "fight the good fight of faith" (1 Tim. 6:12).

I put on the whole armor of God today. Read Ephesians 6:10-12:

Finally, be strong in the Lord and in His mighty power. Put on the full armor of God so that you can take your stand against the devil's schemes. For our struggle is not against flesh and blood, but against the rulers, against the authorities, against the powers of this dark world and against the spiritual forces of evil in the heavenly realms.

Declare that you have your armor on:
- **My belt** I have the belt of truth around my waist (see Eph. 6:14).
- **My breast plate** I am righteous through faith in Jesus Christ. The breast plate is in place (see Eph. 6:14).

I have peace with God through Jesus (see Rom. 5:1).

- **My shoes** I choose to walk in forgiveness and pursue peace (see Rom. 12:18).
- **My shield** I take up the shield of faith to protect me from the enemy's fiery darts.

I quench the fiery darts in Jesus' name through faith in the word of God (see Eph. 6:16).

- **My helmet** I know I am born again and Jesus has changed my life. My helmet of salvation is secure (see Eph. 6:17).
- **My sword** I take the Word of God boldly and confront the powers of darkness in Jesus' name (see Eph. 6:17).

I pray as Your soldier, Lord, with my armor in place.

He is my refuge and my fortress, my God, in whom I trust (Psalm 91:2).

I bind up the demonic strongholds in Jesus' name in _____ (list the person's name) so that he/she can see the truth (see Matt. 18:18).

Lord, I pray that _____ (name someone you are praying for) eyes are opened so that he/she comes to faith in Christ. Unveil their eyes (see 2 Cor. 4:3-4).

I declare that today "I am more than a conqueror" through Jesus Christ.

You will help me come through every obstacle in my life victoriously. "We are more than conquerors through Him who loved us" (Rom. 8:37).

Pray for areas in your life and those you are praying for that you need to fight for (read Neh. 4:14).

Lord, I resist the devil in Jesus' name in this area of my life _____. He must go! (See James 4:7-8.)

Lord, the reason You came was to destroy the work of the enemy. I declare the works of the enemy over _____ is being destroyed in Jesus' name!

"The reason the Son of God appeared was to destroy the devil's work" (1 John 3:8).

Add additional Scriptures to meditate on and prayers to pray below.

_____

_____

_____

_____

In your journal write down how you have used your spiritual armor recently. Take a few minutes to be still before the Lord. Observe if He gives you any more impressions of persons He is calling you to enter into spiritual battle for. Write in your journal those times, both present and past, when you know you have experienced the Lord's deliverance. Also, write down any other prayer requests, answers to prayer, or Scriptures He may be giving to you.

THE KINGDOM ROOM

CHAPTER 12

For Yours is the Kingdom (Matthew 6:13 NKJV).

I thank You, my God, that no matter what is going on in my life at this moment, I am a vital part of Your eternal Kingdom that cannot be shaken!

> *Therefore, since we are receiving a Kingdom that cannot be shaken, let us be thankful, and so worship God acceptably with reverence and awe, for our God is a consuming fire* (Hebrews 12:28-29).

As I enter the Kingdom room, Lord, in everything I say and do today, I ask, "What would Jesus do?"

I thank You that I live as a citizen of Your Kingdom and I am Your son/daughter.

Read Ephesians 1:3-8:

> *Praise be to the God and Father of our Lord Jesus Christ, who has blessed us in the heavenly realms with every spiritual blessing in Christ. For He chose us in Him before the creation of the world to be holy and blameless in His sight. In love He predestined us to be adopted as His sons through Jesus Christ, in accordance with His pleasure and will—to the praise of His glorious grace, which He has freely given us in the One He loves. In Him we have redemption through His blood, the forgiveness of sins, in accordance with the riches of God's grace that He lavished on us with all wisdom and understanding.*

I am a representative of Your Kingdom on earth, Lord.

The Kingdom is within me (see Luke 17:20-21). You make the resources of Heaven available to me when I pray in faith.

Lord, I thank You for Your Kingdom of righteousness, peace, and joy in the Holy Spirit in my life today!

For the Kingdom of God is not a matter of eating and drinking, but of righteousness, peace and joy in the Holy Spirit (Romans 14:17).

I pray for Your Kingdom to become more of a reality in my life and those around me.

Lord, give me an outward focus.

I pray for the nations and Kingdoms of this earth.

I urge, then, first of all, that requests, prayers, intercession and thanksgiving be made for everyone—for kings and all those in authority, that we may live peaceful and quiet lives in all godliness and holiness (1 Timothy 2:1-2).

I pray for the Church of my region, including churches and ministries of many denominations. I pray that we may be one, as the Father and the Son are one (see John 17:21).

Lord, send revival, a visitation of Your Spirit and of Your presence and power to our city, to our region and to our nation. May we experience true transformation.

Here in the Kingdom room, I pray for:

- my family.
- my business.
- my community.
- my church and other churches in my community (for revival).
- my job.
- my loved ones.
- healing for myself and others.
- the gifts of the Spirit to be developed in my life and in the lives of those around me.
- the peace of Jerusalem. (See Psalm 122:6.)
- my president or leader of my nation.
- my spiritual leaders—pastors, elders, deacons.
- for unity in the Kingdom (pray for unity among churches).

Pray through Isaiah 43:5-7. It is a powerful prayer to pray over our families, communities, churches, and nations.

> *Do not be afraid, for I am with you;*
> *I will bring your children from the east*
> *and gather you from the west.*
> *I will say to the north, 'Give them up!'*
> *and to the south, 'Do not hold them back.'*
> *Bring My sons from afar*
> *and My daughters from the ends of the earth—*
> *everyone who is called by My name,*
> *whom I created for My glory,*
> *whom I formed and made."*

Pray this prayer:

"North, (south, east, and west) you have people whom God wills to become a part of the Kingdom of God. Release every person to come into the Kingdom of God and become a part of our church or another church in our community."

Ask God to dispatch angels to minister to those who will inherit salvation from these areas (Heb. 1:13-14). Call them into the Kingdom.

Kingdom praying is not just about our fulfillment, but our transformation and the transformation of those around us (see Luke 12:32; Col. 1:12-14).

Lord, *"All You have made will praise You, O Lord; Your saints will extol You. They will tell of the glory of Your Kingdom and speak of Your might, so that all men may know of Your mighty acts and the glorious splendor of Your Kingdom. Your Kingdom is an everlasting Kingdom, and Your dominion endures through all generations..."* (Psalm 145:10-13).

> *The Lord will rescue me from every evil attack and will bring*
> *me safely to His heavenly Kingdom* (2 Timothy 4:18).

Write the names of the people that you are calling into the Kingdom of God in your prayer journal. Add testimonies, prayer answers, and requests.

People I am praying for regularly _____

_____

_____

_____

Take a few minutes to be still before the Lord. Observe if He gives you any other impressions of areas of your life that you need to acknowledge His Kingdom that cannot be shaken. Write down in your journal times, both present and past, when you know you have experienced the Lord's stability in the midst of uncertain circumstances.

THE POWER ROOM

CHAPTER 13

And the power (Matthew 6:13 NKJV).

Lord, I desperately need the power of God to be manifested in my life today. Holy Spirit, I pray for an infilling of Your Spirit in my life today.

For the Kingdom of God is not a matter of talk but of power (1 Corinthians 4:20).

I need Your power. I pray for a new dimension of the Holy Spirit's power in my life and those I am praying for.

Pray with unceasing prayer and entreaty on every fitting occasion in the Spirit, and be always on the alert to seize opportunities for doing so, with unwearied persistence and entreaty on behalf of all God's people (Ephesians 6:18 Weymouth).

In the power room, take the opportunity to pray, not only in the native language you speak, but also in a spiritual language (your prayer language between God and you, if you have received this gift from the Lord).

I will pray with my spirit, but I will also pray with my mind (1 Corinthians 14:15).

Lord, I know that praying is not about saying the right words. Holy Spirit, help me to pray earnest prayers. "…The prayer of a righteous man is powerful and effective" (James 5:16-18).

When we pray purposefully, God responds powerfully!

I praise You for making Your power available to me.

Yours, O Lord, is the greatness and the power and the glory and the majesty and the splendor, for everything in Heaven and earth is Yours. Yours, O Lord, is the Kingdom; You are exalted as head over all (1 Chronicles 29:11).

Lord, all my work for You depends not on human strength, but by the power of Your Spirit.

Not by might nor by power, but by My Spirit... (Zechariah 4:6)

Lord, I can't solve my problems or the problems of others by myself. I give You full control. I trust You.

My weakness is no obstacle for You! Be strong in the Lord and in His mighty power (see Eph. 6:10).

I praise You for allowing me to be a participant in Your power and making Your power available to me.

Lord, I know I need to be filled with Your Spirit again and again. Fill me again with Your Holy Spirit today.

In Acts 4:31, many of these believers were already filled with the Holy Spirit at Pentecost (see Acts 2). They needed, however, to be filled again.

Lord, just as the early believers knew they needed to be filled again, I too must experience constant renewal. Today, fill me with Your Holy Spirit (see Eph. 5:18) as I live in obedience to You today.

Lord, send a revival. Revive us again!

Will You not revive us again, that Your people may rejoice in You? (Psalm 85:6)

Break up your unplowed ground; for it is time to seek the Lord, until He comes and showers righteousness on you (Hosea 10:12).

Add additional Scriptures to meditate on and prayers to pray below.

_____

_____

_____

In your prayer journal write down how you have been empowered to minister to others recently. List any healings, changed lives, etc. that you have witnessed. Add prayer requests, answers, and other meaningful Scriptures. Write the names of the people that you are calling into the Kingdom of God in your prayer journal. Add testimonies, prayer answers, and requests.

Take a few minutes to be still before the Lord. Observe if He gives you any other impressions of areas of your life or in the lives of others whereby you need to trust in His power to experience victory. Ask the Lord for a fresh infilling of the Holy Spirit today. Add any other Scriptures that you can claim regarding God's power in your life.

THE EXALTATION ROOM

CHAPTER 14

And the glory forever. Amen (Matthew 6:13 NKJV).

Father, here in the exaltation room, I worship You and You alone, for who You are: the Lord of all Lord's and the King of all Kings.

Who is this King of glory? The Lord strong and mighty, the Lord mighty in battle (Psalm 24:8).

Glory and honor are in His presence (1 Chronicles 16:27 KJV).

I am the Lord, that is My name! And My glory will I not give to another, neither My praise to graven images (Isaiah 42:8 AMP).

I exalt You and worship You with my heart.

...true worshipers will worship the Father in Spirit and truth, for they are the kind of worshipers the Father seeks. God is Spirit, and His worshipers must worship in Spirit and in truth (John 4:23-24).

For from Him and through Him and to Him are all things. To Him be the glory forever! (Romans 11:36)

Lord, I praise and worship You with my whole spirit, soul, and body. You live in my praises.

...You are enthroned as the Holy One; you are the praise of Israel (Psalm 22:3).

May the praise of God be in their mouths and a double-edged sword in their hands, to inflict vengeance on the nations and punishment on the peoples, to bind their kings with fetters, their nobles with shackles of iron (Psalm 149:6-8).

Lord, I look forward to worshiping You throughout all eternity.

A great multitude that no one could count, from every nation, tribe, people and language, standing before the throne and in front of the Lamb. They were wearing white robes and were holding palm branches in their hands. And they cried out in a loud voice: 'Salvation belongs to our God, who sits on the throne, and to the Lamb' (Revelation 7:9-11).

Lord, may my life of obedience be a sacrifice of praise and worship to You!

Through Jesus, therefore, let us continually offer to God a sacrifice of praise—the fruit of lips that confess His name. And do not forget to do good and to share with others, for with such sacrifices God is pleased (Hebrews 13:15-16).

Therefore, I urge you, brothers, in view of God's mercy, to offer your bodies as living sacrifices, holy and pleasing to God—this is your spiritual act of worship (Romans 12:1).

Lord, expand my vision of yourself. You are able to do immeasurable more than all I can ask or imagine, according to Your power that is at work within me (see Eph. 3:20).

I will express myself in worship to You in the exaltation room.

- Kneeling. (See Psalm 95:6.)
- Standing and worshiping. (See Revelation 7:9-10.)
- Lifting up our hands. (See 1 Timothy 2:8.)
- Being still. (See Psalm 46:10.)
- Praising Him with instruments. (See Psalm 150:3,5.)
- Dancing. (See Psalm 149:3.)
- Singing new songs. (See Psalm 149:1.)
- Clapping and shouting. (See Psalm 47:1.)

- Speaking in psalms and hymns and spiritual songs and making melody in our hearts: Use your favorite worship CD and bask in the Lord's presence.
- Singing to the Lord: When you praise the Lord, the enemy takes flight! (See 2 Chronicles 20:22.)

Add additional Scriptures to meditate on and prayers to pray below.

_____

_____

_____

_____

Listen for the Lord to speak to you about anything else He wants to tell you during your time of prayer. Write in your prayer journal your own words of worship to the Creator God whom you serve. Declare His Lordship over every area of your life. Add answers to prayer, prayer requests, and meaningful scriptures. Take a few minutes to be still before the Lord. Observe if He gives you any other impressions of His greatness and His power to exalt Him for who He is. Add any other Scriptures that you can use to exalt Him as your Lord and King.

Remember the words of Martin Luther, "Do not leave your prayer without having said or thought, 'Very well, God has heard my prayer, this I know as a certainty and a truth.' This is what Amen means."[1]

ENDNOTE

1. Martin Luther, *A Simple Way to Pray* (Louisville, KY: Westminster Knox Press, 2000), 29.

Using the Small Group Lessons

These outlines are designed for small group teachers to use as they lead their group into building their own personal house of prayer. Questions throughout the teaching facilitate discussion and interaction in the group. The length of the lessons may be customized to suit your time frame.

SMALL GROUP LESSON—CHAPTER 1

Lord, Teach Us To Pray

1. **Are you as consistent as you want to be in spending time with Jesus?**
    a. The disciples saw Jesus praying often and consistently (see Mark 1:35; Luke 5:16; Luke 6:12; Luke 22:39).
    b. They wanted to learn to pray. In Luke 11:1-4, one of His disciples came to Jesus with a request, "Lord, teach us to pray..." (Luke 11:1).
    c. Ask someone to hold you accountable in spending time with the Lord each day.
2. **Jesus gave the disciples the Lord's Prayer as a model** (see Matt. 6:9-13).
    a. Why do you want to learn to pray?
    b. How has prayer at times felt legalistic to you?
3. **House of prayer.**
    a. In the Old Testament, God's house was a place set apart for sacred use—a place to access for all those who sought God.
    b. In the New Testament, there are no special places or buildings for prayer. There is free access wherever people find themselves (see Acts 17:24).
    c. In the Old Testament, there were holy places, but in the New Testament, God's people are holy (see 1 Pet. 2:9).
    d. There is no literal house of prayer, God resides within His people (see 1 Cor. 3:16).
    e. Becoming a house of prayer is a metaphor that applies to us individually when we come to prayer.
4. **Joy in our house of prayer.**
    a. Prayer times alone with God each day should be filled with great joy! (See Isa. 56:7.)
    b. Describe a time you found joy in prayer.

5.   **Use the Lord's Prayer as a guide.**
     a.   "Enter into His gates..." (Ps. 100:4). Envision yourself entering into a courtyard house with twelve rooms.
     b.   In the next lessons, we will learn twelve different ways to pray based on the Lord's Prayer.

PRAYER TIME

Pray for each other to find more joy and consistency in prayer.

SMALL GROUP LESSON—CHAPTER 2

Entering Into Our House of Prayer

1. The "password" for coming through the door and into the courtyard is "thanksgiving and praise" (see Ps. 100:4-5).

   a. Gates were the entrance into the Old Testament temple. In the New Testament, we ourselves are the temple (see 1 Pet. 2:5).

   b. Praise and thanksgiving are linked. Thanks is the basis of our praise.

   c. To praise God means to respond to God for what He has done.

2. **Praise God for specific things He has done in your life. Share with the group.**

3. **Sacrifice of praise** (see Heb. 13:15).

   a. Praise is a sacrifice that we offer to God because we want to please Him. Tell of a time you offered praise to God when you didn't feel like it (it was a sacrifice).

   b. Praising and being thankful tells God that we believe He is in control of our circumstances (see Rom. 8:28).

   c. Share an experience where you offered praise to God when you didn't feel like it (it was a sacrifice).

4. **God inhabits the praises of His people** (see Ps. 22:3).

   a. God "dwells" in the atmosphere of His praise. Praise actually brings us into the presence and power of God!

   b. By meditating on the word of God and praising God for His promises, we begin to see ourselves from the Lord's perspective, instead of from our perspectives.

   c. Give an example of a time praise brought you into the presence of God.

5. **Attitude of thanksgiving** (see Phil. 4:6).

   a. We lay our past and present before the Lord and thank Him for who He is and what He has done.

b.   Peace comes when we have an attitude of thanksgiving (see Phil. 4:7-8).

6.   **The power of praise and thanksgiving crowds out criticism, and helps to defeat depression and fear** (see Isa. 26:3; Ps. 42:5).

a.   Did praising God ever help you defeat criticism, depression, or fear? Give an example.

QUIET TIME

Can you identify any current fears or an intimacy issue that would inhibit you from entering into His courts of praise and prayer? Write them down and ask God for His solutions.

SMALL GROUP LESSON—CHAPTER 3

The Family Room; *Our Father in Heaven*

1. **God wants to lavish His love on us!**
   a. He calls us His children (see 1 John 3:1).
   b. As believers in Jesus, we are a part of a spiritual family, the family of God.
   c. Have you experienced the love of your heavenly Daddy?
2. **If we are to have a healthy prayer life, we must be certain of our Father's love for us and live in close relationship to Him.**
   a. The secret of Jesus' love for us: "As the Father has loved Me, I also have loved you..." (see John 15:9).
   b. John was secure in Jesus' love.
3. **We can come boldly to the throne of grace and obtain mercy in our time of need** (see Heb. 4:16).
   a. Every morning you can walk into the family room where your heavenly Father tells you how much He loves you!
   b. There is nothing you can do to deserve it. You are fully accepted.
4. **Applying God's word in prayer**
   a. God's word is a love letter to us.
   b. It's filled with living power for our lives (see Heb. 4:12).
   c. How have I applied God's word to my life recently?
5. **Take some time to read from the Bible and receive encouragement, wisdom, and instruction from a Daddy who loves us perfectly.**
   a. Read for a few minutes from the Psalms, the Proverbs, or from the book of John. Turn them into prayer.
   b. Then take a minute or so to be silent and see if the Lord gives any more impressions of His love for you. Share with the group.

SMALL GROUP LESSON—CHAPTER 4

The Adoration Room; *Hallowed be Your name*

1. **How do you describe God? His name helps us.**
   a. God told Moses, "I am who I am" (Exod. 3:14).
   b. God's name is not just His name—it is who He is.
2. **God is holy** (see Exod. 15:11; Isaiah 6:3; Psalm 103:1).
   a. *Holy* means "to sanctify or set apart."
   b. God is totally *separate* or *different* from what we are (Isa. 55:8).
3. **God's name is above all others** (see Phil. 2:9-11).
   a. The most powerful Name in Heaven and earth has been given to us "if we believe."
   b. Believe what? Read John 20:31: "But these are written that you may believe that Jesus is the Christ, the Son of God, and that by believing you may have life in His name."
   c. Because God is holy, we can reign in life through Christ. "For if, by the trespass of the one man, death reigned through that one man, how much more will those who receive God's abundant provision of grace and of the gift of righteousness reign in life through the one man, Jesus Christ" (Rom. 5:17).
4. **Speak the names of God in prayer.**
   a. The names of God help us to understand His character.
   b. Read over the list of the names of God in Chapter 4, and invite Him to be those things to you.
5. **Adoration is the purest kind of prayer.**
   a. Spend time in prayer as a group. Tell Him you love Him!
   b. Reflect on His greatness.

SMALL GROUP LESSON—CHAPTER 5

The Declaration Room; *Your Kingdom come*

1. **In the declaration room we have an abiding knowledge that God reigns in our hearts and transforms us into His likeness.**
    a. God's Kingdom is set up in our hearts (see Mark 1:14-15).
    b. Have individuals describe how God has changed them from the inside out.
    c. Nicodemus had a hard time understanding that God would change hearts (see John 3:3).
2. **Declare God's word over our families, churches, communities, nations, circumstances, and finances.**
    a. God's Kingdom and will are identical to God's word.
    b. Read God's word aloud. It's filled with living power (see Heb. 4:12).
3. **God has a specific plan for our lives.**
    a. Many blessings go unclaimed because we believe the lies of the enemy.
    b. The opportunities to apply His promises are endless (see Phil. 4:13).
4. **Jesus invites us to labor with Him in His Kingdom.**
    a. He is as active here on earth as He is in Heaven.
    b. "May Your Kingdom come" declares that the world is transformed into a place where God reigns (see Matt. 6:10; Luke 11:12).
    c. We stand in the victory Christ has won for us and walk in righteousness, peace, and joy (see Rom. 14:17).
5. **Let's declare the word over our lives.**
    a. Declare Hebrews 13:5; James 4:7; Luke 4:18.
    b. See Appendix A, and declare these verses.
    c. Praying for God's Kingdom to come invites a drastic restructuring of our lives and priorities.

PRAYER TIME

Spend time declaring God's word over your family, church, community, nations, circumstances, and finances.

SMALL GROUP LESSON—CHAPTER 6

The Surrender Room; *Your will be done, on earth as it is in Heaven*

1. **Surrendering is trusting the details of our lives to God.**
   a. We invite God into our lives here on earth.
   b. Surrendering means to yield ownership, to relinquish control over what we consider ours: our property, time, rights.
   c. In what ways have you surrendered your time to God? Have you ever demanded that God perform as a magician because you wanted instant solutions? Share with the group.
   d. Even Jesus surrendered His desire to "let this cup pass." He was willing to surrender that desire. (See Matthew 26:39.)
2. **Praying that God's will be done on earth as it is in Heaven is a plea for transformation of our lives.**
   a. Seek first His Kingdom (see Matt. 6:33).
   b. As we surrender our lives, His Kingdom comes.
3. **Surrendering may involve waiting.**
   a. Instructions for waiting on the Lord (see Ps. 62:1; Ps. 130:6; Isa. 40:31).
   b. This is not day-dreaming but an exercise that demands an alert mind.
4. **If we want daily guidance, we must acknowledge Him as Lord over all** (Prov. 3:5-6).
   a. Jesus instructs us to rest in quiet submission to His will (see Matt. 11:28-30).
   b. Learning to rest is "casting our cares on Him" (1 Pet. 5:7).
5. **Surrendering is being content.**
   a. Have you learned to be content? (See Philippians 4:11.)
   b. We don't delight in the circumstances, but recognize that God is in charge and has it under control.

QUIET TIME

Encourage each person to surrender themselves to the Lord in a quiet time of prayer.

SMALL GROUP LESSON—CHAPTER 7

The Provision Room; *Give us today our daily bread*

1. **God wants to provide for us!**
    a. "You do not have, because you do not ask" (James 4:2).
    b. God is committed to providing our daily needs as we seek His Kingdom first.
2. **God provided daily manna for Israelites. It could not be stored.**
    a. Yesterday's experience with God was yesterday's.
    b. Each day we have to draw closer to God for our daily nourishment.
3. **Don't preoccupy yourselves with food and clothing** (see Matt. 6:25-34).
    a. We can trust Him! Don't be anxious (see Phil. 4:6).
    b. Trust not only for our own needs but for the needs of others.
4. **Abundant supply**
    a. God's supply is limitless (see Eph. 3:20).
    b. *El Shaddai* is God of "more than enough."
    c. Abundant blessing is the nature of God (see Mal. 3:10-12; 3 John 1:2).
5. **Let your requests be known**
    a. Ask! (See Luke 11:9-10.) God wants to give (see Matt. 7:11).
    b. Answer may be "yes, no, wait."
6. **All we have belongs to God.**
    a. We are stewards (see 1 Cor. 4:1-2,7).
    b. Systematic giving—the tithe (see Gen. 14:18-20; Prov. 3:9-10; 1 Cor. 16:2).
7. **Serving God has benefits!**
    a. Read Deuteronomy 28 for a list of blessings if we obey!

SHARE WITH EACH OTHER

Tell of a time when God provided for you.

SMALL GROUP LESSON—CHAPTER 8

The Forgiveness Room; *Forgive us our debts*

1. **What is sin?**
    a. *Sin* is "missing the bull's eye."
    b. It's not just robbing a bank or murdering someone; it can take the form of a lie, gossip, and so forth.
    c. Anything off the center of God's best for us is sin.
    d. The Lord's Prayer not only mentions our sin, it tells of God's forgiveness.
2. **Forgiveness.**
    a. Jesus forgives or wipes clean our sin by His blood shed on the cross (see 1 John 1:7).
    b. God loves to forgive sin when we repent.
3. **Sins are not remembered.**
    a. God forgives our sins—never to remember or mention them again.
    b. As far as the east is from the west, so far He has removed our sins from us (see Ps. 103:12).
4. **Confession.**
    a. The Lord's Prayer also teaches us how to move from sin to forgiveness.
    b. We ask for it! We admit our guilt and need for God's forgiveness. Confession verbalizes our spiritual shortcomings.
    c. Unconfessed sin will weigh us down (see Ps. 66:18-20).
    d. Confessing is a daily activity because we are not perfect (see 1 John 1:8-10; 2:1-2).
5. **False guilt is leftover negative feelings from our sinful past.**
    a. Have you ever struggled with false guilt? Ask individuals to share their stories.
    b. Claim these verses (see 1 John 1:9; Ps. 103:12).

DISCUSSION TIME

Share a personal forgiveness story with someone in the group.

Share with someone how healing occurred as a result of confessing sin in your life.

SMALL GROUP LESSON—CHAPTER 9

The Freedom Room; *As we also have forgiven our debtors*

1. **We must forgive those who have sinned against us in order for God to forgive us** (see Matt. 6:14-15).
   a. Example: Parable of the servant (see Matt. 18).
   b. If we don't forgive, God will deliver us to the "torturers" (see Matt. 18:34-35). Unforgiveness leaves the door open for the devil!
2. **Why we need to forgive.**
   a. Keep short accounts because a root grows up to cause trouble (see Heb. 12:15).
   b. We are a prisoner of the one who has hurt us.
3. **Allow God to defend us.**
   a. Have you ever been falsely accused? What did you do?
   b. Read Numbers 5:11-20.
   c. Respond in a spirit of humility.
4. **Become offense proof.**
   a. Release those who have offended us, and we can go free!
   b. Forgiveness and prayer is the key (see Matt. 6:9-15; Mark 11:24-26).
5. **Turn accusation into intercession.**
   a. We must find freedom in five areas of accusation from the enemy: The devil accuses: us to God, God to us, us to others, others to us, and us to ourselves (condemnation).
   b. Mercy triumphs (see James 2:13). A merciful person rejoices in opportunities to show mercy rather than requiring strict justice.
6. **Forgiveness is ongoing.**
   a. Once you've dealt with the past, constant infractions occur in the present.
   b. We must constantly forgive when we are hurt or our pride is wounded.

DISCUSS

How has forgiveness taught you how to live with others?

Describe a time a root of bitterness grew and you became a prisoner of the one who hurt you.

SMALL GROUP LESSON—CHAPTER 10

The Protection Room; *And lead us not into temptation*

1. **What can we do when we are tempted?**
   a. "Pray that you may not enter into temptation" (Luke 22:40 NKJV).
   b. "The spirit indeed *is* willing, but the flesh *is* weak" (Matt. 26:41 NKJV).
   c. Jesus understands. He was tempted (see Heb. 4:15-16).
2. **Don't give in!** (See James 1:13-15.)
   a. Temptation is not sin.
   b. It becomes sin when we allow it to gain control of our thoughts and actions.
3. **Temptation comes from satan.** (See Hebrews 4:15.)
   a. See also Mark 1:13; 1 Thessalonians 3:5.
   b. Prayer is essential in resisting temptation.
4. **God will provide a way out of temptation.** (See 1 Corinthians 10:13.)
   a. The path to victory is to admit defeat.
   b. Stop trying to fight on our own power and come to God (see Zech. 4:6). Make it a matter of prayer.
5. **God's "protection promises" do not fall short.**
   a. Three main areas of temptation: coveting, lust of our eyes, and pride (see 1 John 2:16).
   b. Take time to listen to the Holy Spirit. Receive His promises of protection. Read Psalm 91 and claim each promise for yourself and those you are praying for.
6. **God commands His angels to keep you safe from danger and harm.** (See Psalm 91.)
   a. God will keep you from falling.
   b. Claim His protection at home, at school, on the job, on vacation.

SHARE TOGETHER

Share with someone an area of your life for which you need prayer to keep you from temptation.

Describe a time when the Lord protected you and kept you from falling into sin.

SMALL GROUP LESSON—CHAPTER 11

The Warfare Room; *But deliver us from the evil one*

1. **We are engaged in a spiritual conflict with evil.**
   a. We are guaranteed victory through Christ's death, but must wage spiritual warfare (see Rom. 8:13).
   b. Fight the good fight (see 1 Tim. 6:12).
   c. Enemy trying to devour and deceive us (see 1 Pet. 5:8; 2 Cor. 11:14).
2. **How does a Christian wage war?**
   a. Be strong in the Lord, put on armor (see Eph. 6:10-12).
   b. Our fight is not with people, but with the powers of darkness.
   c. It's not us against the devil, it's us and God against the devil.
   d. We take the rhema word of God for our specific situation and use it as an offensive weapon to cause the enemy to flee.
3. **Why spiritual armor?**
   a. God has called us to stand firm in the midst of attacks from the enemy and our sinful natures.
   b. Get up in the morning and declare that your spiritual armor is in place. You are righteous (breastplate in place); you have the shield of faith in place so the fiery darts of the enemy cannot penetrate. Helmet of salvation is secure, and so forth (see Eph. 6:10-18).
4. **Binding strongholds.**
   a. Our words alone are not a magic formula to control the spirit realm, but "binding on earth what is bound in Heaven" reveals a powerful authority Christ gives us to declare what He is doing and has already done (see 2 Cor. 4:3-4; Matt. 18:18).
   b. As directed by the Holy Spirit, we can pray and bind strongholds in people's lives so they will be free to hear the Gospel and respond to Jesus.

   c.   With such Christ initiated prayer, we have authority to bind up the work of the enemy that is influencing our lives or others' lives (see Matt. 12:29-30; Mark 16:17).

5.   **We can be victorious** (Rom. 8:37).

   a.   Fight for your family and those you are praying for (see Neh. 4:14; James 4:7-8).

   b.   The reason Jesus came was to destroy the devil's work (see 1 John 3:8-9).

DISCUSSION

Have you ever fought against something that limited God's work in your life? Explain.

Tell of a time when you "put on" a specific piece of armor and used it as an offensive weapon to cause the enemy to flee.

SMALL GROUP LESSON—CHAPTER 12

The Kingdom Room; *For yours is the Kingdom*

1. **"Yours is the Kingdom" refers to the presence and power of God's actual rule.**
    a. As God exercises His authority on earth, the Kingdom of God is here (see Mark 1:15).
    b. When we recognize God's rule over our lives, we take on His values. "What would Jesus do?"
2. **Declare that the Kingdom is the Lord's.**
    a. We are citizens of God's Kingdom; He has chosen us (see Eph. 1:3-8).
    b. The Kingdom of God is within us (see Luke 17:20-21). You take the Kingdom with you wherever you go.
    c. If there is a lack of righteousness, peace, and joy in your life, there is a lack of His Kingdom (see Rom. 14:17).
3. **God's Kingdom includes all of His people in the world who name His name.**
    a. God's Kingdom is where the love of God is shown to the world, where the hungry are fed, sick healed, and so forth.
    b. All of this helps increase the presence of the heavenly Kingdom here on earth.
4. **Pray Kingdom prayers.**
    a. Kingdom praying is praying for things that matter for eternity.
    b. It is being concerned about the things God is concerned about.
    c. Believers everywhere expand His Kingdom through the work of prayer and intercession (see 1 Tim. 2:1-3).
    d. Pray for family, business, marriages, jobs, government, loved ones, healing, gifts of the Spirit, for example.
    e. Be specific in your prayers!
    f. Isaiah 43 can be turned into a powerful prayer.

g. Praying is about our transformation and the transformation of those around us.

DISCUSSION AND PRAYER

How did your values and behavior change when you recognized God's rule over your life and that you are a part of His unshakeable Kingdom?

Do you see a lack of righteousness, peace, and joy in your life? This is a lack of His Kingdom. Pray Kingdom prayers for transformation in your life and other's lives.

SMALL GROUP LESSON—CHAPTER 13

The Power Room; *And the power*

1. **"Kingdom of God is not a matter of talk but of power"** (1 Cor. 4:20).
2. **We need to be plugged into the power source of the Holy Spirit.**
    a. Pray for a new dimension of the Holy Spirit's power in your life.
    b. Pray in the Spirit (see Eph. 6:18).
    c. With the power of God evident in our lives, we are empowered to minister to others (see Acts 1:4-5, 8).
3. **Power of prayer**
    a. Praying with power can take various forms. Our own language or our spiritual language (see 1 Cor. 14:15).
    b. "Prayer of a righteous man..." (James 5:16-18).
    c. God will strengthen you with power through His Spirit in your inner being (see Eph. 3:16).
4. **Praying is not about saying the right words but the power comes from the Holy Spirit helping us to pray.**
    a. God responds powerfully when we pray purposefully.
    b. God made His power available to you (see 1 Chron. 29:11; Eph. 6:10).
5. **In prayer, we express our commitment and trust in God.**
    a. "God does everything by prayer and nothing without it."—John Wesley
    b. We are participants in His power just as they were in the book of Acts, Chapter 2, when they were filled with the Holy Spirit.
    c. This power comes as a result of prayer.
    d. Man's weakness is no obstacle for God (see Zech. 4:6).

PRAYER TIME

Pray for each other—for a new dimension of the Holy Spirit's power.

SMALL GROUP LESSON—CHAPTER 14

The Exaltation Room; *And the glory forever. Amen.*

1. **Exalting God is giving Him all the glory and praise that only He deserves.**
   a. "Who is this King?" (Ps. 24:8).
   b. "Glory and honor are in His presence" (1 Chron. 16:27).
   c. "My glory I will not give to another" (Isa. 42:8).
2. **Our worship focuses on who He is—His person.**
   a. Everyone worships something.
   b. We must worship with our hearts (see John 4:23-24).
3. **We need to be involved privately in praise and worship in our time alone with God.**
   a. Take the Book of Psalms and sing and pray them as you worship God.
   b. We worship in preparation for Heaven (see Ps. 115:17).
   c. When we realize what God has done for us, we can't help but get caught up in praise and worship.
   d. The enemy takes flight when we worship (see 2 Chron. 20:22).
4. **Ways to express worship**
   a. Kneel. (See Psalm 95:6.)
   b. Stand and worship. (See Revelation 7:9-10.)
   c. Lift up our hands. (See First Timothy 2:8.)
   d. Be still before the Lord. (See Psalm 46:10.)
   e. Praise Him with instruments. (See Psalm 150:3,5.)
   f. Dance. (See Psalm 149:3.)
   g. Sing new songs. (See Psalm 149:1.)
   h. Clap and shout. (See Psalm 47:1.)
   i. Speak in psalms and hymns and spiritual songs. (See Ephesians 5:19.)
5. **Expand your vision of God!**
   a. God is able to do immeasurably more than all we ask or imagine... (see Eph. 3:20).

WORSHIP TOGETHER AS A GROUP

Spend time worshiping God in ways you don't normally worship Him. Move out of your comfort zone!

Small Group Lesson —Chapter 15

Building Your Personal House of Prayer; *Let's get started*

1. **We are not alone; we are part of the family of God!**
   a. Building our prayer life is not about rules, but relationship.
   b. Building a personal house of prayer through praying the Lord's Prayer is simply a guideline. Prayer is about friendship with God.
2. **Praying through the twelve rooms helps maintain a well-rounded prayer life.**
   a. Follow the Holy Spirit's direction.
   b. Depending on what you need, you may spend more time in some rooms than others each day.
3. **Spend some time in your small group listening for His voice.**
   a. God may surprise us in how He speaks to us (see Job 33:14).
   b. He may speak through the inner witness of the Holy Spirit, His word, circumstances, other people, dreams, visions, for example.
4. **God desires a two-way communication** (see Gen. 3:8).
   a. The more consistent we are in spending time with the Lord, the deeper our relationship will grow (see Jer. 29:12-13).
   b. Come trusting God to change us, through prayer.
5. **Jesus needed a touch from God each day** (see Mark 1:35) **and so do we.**
   a. He knew He needed to slow down all the busyness and distractions in life to spend time in prayer.
   b. Through prayer we gain a clearer sense of who we are and what we are to do.
6. **Find a prayer spot.**
   a. Schedule time with God each day.

b.   Have a specific place to pray undisturbed (see Matt. 6:6).

c.   Praying through the twelve rooms of prayer is a sort of "physical fitness regimen" that allows flexibility and spontaneity as you develop it.

SMALL GROUP LESSON—EPILOGUE

Revive Us Again!: *Revivals are birthed in prayer*

1. **Look at the comparison of the percentages of Bible-based believers between the generations.**
   a. Do you agree that America is in desperate need of revival?
   b. What is revival? (See Ps. 85:6; Hosea 10:12.)
2. **The Great Awakening came out of a time of great spiritual darkness.**
   a. Discuss the revival efforts of John and Charles Wesley and George Whitefield in England during the mid 1700s. What was the common theme?
   b. In colonial America (late 1700s), Jonathan Edwards of Massachusetts and Francis Asbury were instrumental in bringing approximately one-third of the population of the American colonies to a salvation experience.
3. **The power of prayer dominated America's revivalism.**
   a. Charles Finney's preaching sometimes resulted in entire towns being converted.
   b. Jeremiah Lanphier started a businessman's prayer meeting in downtown New York City.
4. **Read how the revivals in the 1800s were birthed by prayer.**
   a. Discuss the 1859 revival in Wales and how it impacted America. How did the press respond?
   b. How long did Evan Roberts pray before he saw a move of God's Spirit?
5. **Great moves of God are always preceded by prayer and obedience** (see Acts 2:41; Acts 5:1).
   a. If we really believed prayer changes things, we would be praying.

    b.   Pray for the Holy Spirit to show anything in our lives (including prayerlessness) that could hinder us from experiencing revival.

6. Pray for the harvest!

    a.   Acts 2:17-18 declares that God will visit His people. This Scripture was fulfilled at Pentecost, yet God desires an even greater fulfillment as thousands more turn to Him and receive an outpouring of His Spirit.

    b.   Let's pray!

Who I Am in Christ

Lord, I declare the following Scriptures over my life so that I know without a doubt who I am in You:

I am now God's child (see 1 John 3:2).

I am born of the imperishable seed of God's Word (see 1 Pet. 1:23).

I am loved by Christ and freed from my sins (see Rev. 1:5).

I am forgiven all my sins (see Eph. 1:7).

I am justified from all things (see Acts 13:39).

I am the righteousness of God (see 2 Cor. 5:21).

I am free from all condemnation (see Rom. 8:1).

I can forget the past (see Phil. 3:13).

I am a new creature (see 2 Cor. 5:17).

I am the temple of the Holy Spirit (see 1 Cor. 6:19).

I am redeemed from the curse of the law (see Gal. 3:13).

I am reconciled to God (see 2 Cor. 5:18).

I am beloved of God (see 1 John 4:10).

I am a saint and loved by God (see Rom. 1:7).

I am holy and without blame before Him (see Eph. 1:4).

I am the head and not the tail (see Deut. 28:13).

I am called of God by the grace given in Christ (see 1 Tim. 1:9).

I am brought near by the blood of Christ (see Eph. 2:13).

I have been given fullness in Christ (see Col. 2:10).

I am delivered from the power of darkness (see Col. 1:13).

I am an ambassador for Christ (see 2 Cor. 5:20).

I am the salt of the earth (see Matt. 5:13).

I am the light of the world (see Matt. 5:14).

I am dead to sin (see Rom.6:2).

I am alive to God (see Rom. 6:11).

I am raised up with Christ and seated in heavenly realms (see Eph. 2:6).

I am a king and a priest to God (see Rev. 1:6).

I am loved with an everlasting love (see Jer. 31:3).

I am an heir of God and a joint heir with Christ (see Rom. 8:17).

I am qualified to share in the inheritance of the Kingdom (see Col. 1:12).

I am more than a conqueror (see Rom. 8:37).

I am healed by the wounds of Jesus (see 1 Pet. 2:24).

I am built on the foundation of the apostles and prophets, with Jesus Christ Himself as the chief cornerstone (see Eph. 2:20).

I am in Christ Jesus by God's act (see 1 Cor. 1:30).

I am kept by God's power (see 1 Pet. 1:5).

I am sealed with the promised Holy Spirit (see Eph. 1:13).

I have everlasting life (see John 5:24).

I am crucified with Christ nevertheless I live (see Gal. 2:20).

I am a partaker of the divine nature (see 2 Pet. 1:4).

I have been given all things that pertain to life (see 2 Pet. 1:3).

I have been blessed with every spiritual blessing (see Eph. 1:3).

I have peace with God (see Rom. 5:1).

I am a chosen royal priest (see 1 Pet. 2:9).

I can do all things through Christ (see Phil. 4:13).

I have all my needs met by God according to His riches in glory in Christ Jesus (see Phil. 4:19).

I shall do even greater works than Christ Jesus (see John 14:12).

I am being kept strong and blameless to the end (see 1 Cor. 1:8).

I am chosen by Him (see 1 Thess. 1:4).

I overcome the world (see 1 John 5:4).

I have a guaranteed inheritance (see Eph. 1:14).

I am a fellow citizen in God's household (see Eph. 2:19).

Christ's truth has set me free (see John 8:32).

I always triumph in Christ (see 2 Cor. 2:14).

I am in Jesus Christ's hands (see John 10:28).

I am holy, without blemish and free from accusation (see Col. 1:22).

Christ in me is the hope of glory (see Col. 1:27).

I am anointed by the Holy one (see 1 John 2:20).

God's love is lavished upon me (see 1 John 3:1).

He is able to keep me from falling and present me without fault (see Jude 24).

I am God's house (see Heb. 3:6).

God has given me a spirit of power, of love, and of self discipline (see 2 Tim. 1:7).

I am convinced that He is able to guard what I have entrusted to Him (see 2 Tim. 1:12).

He has considered me faithful and appointed me to His service (see 1 Tim. 1:12).

I am justified by faith (see Rom. 3:28).

The Spirit Himself intercedes for me (see Rom. 8:26).

Inwardly I am being renewed day by day (see 2 Cor. 4:16).

For freedom Christ has set me free (see Gal. 5:1).

I am held together by Him (see Col. 1:17).

I have the mind of Christ (see 1 Cor. 2:16).

The Lord's Prayer

Matthew 6:9-13

NEW INTERNATIONAL VERSION

Our Father in Heaven, hallowed be Your name,
Your Kingdom come,
Your will be done on earth as it is in Heaven.
Give us today our daily bread.
Forgive us our debts, as we also have forgiven our debtors.

KING JAMES VERSION

Our Father which art in Heaven, Hallowed be thy name.
Thy Kingdom come,
Thy will be done in earth, as it is in Heaven.
Give us this day our daily bread. And forgive us our debts,
as we forgive our debtors.
And lead us not into temptation, but deliver us from evil:
For thine is the Kingdom, and the power, and the glory,
*   for ever. Amen.*

NEW LIVING TRANSLATION

Our Father in Heaven, may Your name be kept holy. May Your
Kingdom come soon. May Your will be done on earth, as it is in Heaven.
Give us today the food we need, and forgive us our sins, as we have for-
given those who sin against us. And don't let us yield to temptation, but
rescue us from the evil one. For yours is the Kingdom and the power and
the glory forever. Amen.

New King James Version

Our Father in Heaven, Hallowed be Your name. Your Kingdom come. Your will be done on earth as it is in Heaven. Give us this day our daily bread. And forgive us our debts, As we forgive our debtors. And do not lead us into temptation, But deliver us from the evil one. For Yours is the Kingdom and the power and the glory forever. Amen.

About the Author and Ministry

Larry Kreider initially served for 15 years as senior pastor of DOVE Christian Fellowship in Pennsylvania, which grew from a single small group to over 2,300 in ten years. Today, DOVE Christian Fellowship International (DCFI) believers are found meeting in more than 150 congregations throughout the United States, Central and South America, Caribbean, Canada, Europe, Africa, Asia, and the South Pacific.

Larry started in ministry in 1971, helping found a youth ministry that targeted unchurched youth in his community of northern Lancaster County, Pennsylvania. Dozens came to faith in Christ and he was soon teaching a large group of young people each week. DCFI grew out of the ensuing need for a flexible New Testament-style church that could assist new believers. In small groups, new believers found a place to experience and demonstrate Christianity built on relationships. They could readily share their lives with each other, grow up spiritually, and reach out with the healing love of Jesus to the world.

Continuing over the past two decades, Larry pursues his vision to build the church with a small group focus in the nations of the world and put prayer into action to pave the way for revival in the nations. He is a featured speaker at conferences and has traveled extensively training Christian leaders and believers from many different denominations and churches.

Larry has written several books, including *House to House, The Cry For Spiritual Fathers & Mothers, House Church Networks, Starting a House Church, a twelve book Biblical Foundation Series, Helping You Build Cell Churches Manual, The Biblical Role of Elders for*

Today's Church, Hearing God, and *Authentic Spiritual Mentoring.* Larry also writes articles for Christian periodicals, including *Ministries Today, Cell Group Journal, Kairos* Magazine, *Morning Star Journal, House2House* Magazine, and others.

Larry and his wife, LaVerne, have been married for 36 years and make their home in Lititz, Pennsylvania. They have four children and three grandchildren.

Larry would love to hear your story describing ways your prayer life has been impacted by reading this book. Please e-mail your story to yourstory@dcfi.org.

Contact information for seminars and speaking engagements:
Larry Kreider, International Director
DOVE Christian Fellowship International
11 Toll Gate Road
Lititz, PA 17543
Tel: 717-627-1996
Fax: 717-627-4004
Website: www.dcfi.org
E-mail: LarryK@dcfi.org

Resources from DCFI

Hearing God 30 Different Ways by Larry Kreider

The Lord speaks to us in ways we often miss, including through the Bible, prayer, circumstances, spiritual gifts, conviction, His character, His peace, and even in times of silence. Take 30 days and discover how God's voice can become familiar to you as you develop a loving relationship with Him. 224 pages: $14.99: ISBN: 978-1-886973-76-3

The Cry for Spiritual Fathers & Mothers by Larry Kreider

Returning to the biblical truth of spiritual parenting so believers are not left fatherless and disconnected. How loving, seasoned spiritual fathers and mothers help spiritual children reach their potential. 186 pages: $12.99: ISBN: 978-1-886973-42-8

The Biblical Role of Elders for Today's Church by Larry Kreider, Ron Myer, Steve Prokopchak, and Brian Sauder

New Testament principles for equipping church leadership teams: Why leadership is needed, what their qualifications and responsibilities are, how they should be chosen, how elders function as spiritual fathers and mothers, how they are to make decisions, resolve conflicts, and more. 274 pages: $12.99: ISBN: 978-1-886973-62-6

BIBLICAL FOUNDATION SERIES

This series by Larry Kreider covers basic Christian doctrine. Practical illustrations accompany the easy-to-understand format. Use for small group teachings (48 in all), a mentoring relationship, or daily devotional. Each book has 64 pages: $4.99 each, 12 Book Set: $39: ISBN: 978-1-886973-18-3

BIBLICAL FOUNDATION TITLES

1. Knowing Jesus Christ as Lord
2. The New Way of Living
3. New Testament Baptisms
4. Building for Eternity
5. Living in the Grace of God
6. Freedom from the Curse
7. Learning to Fellowship with God
8. What is the Church?
9. Authority and Accountability
10. God's Perspective on Finances
11. Called to Minister
12. The Great Commission
    Available in Spanish!

HOUSE-TO-HOUSE by Larry Kreider

How God called a small fellowship to become an international movement. DOVE Christian Fellowship International has grown into a family of churches networking throughout the world. 206 pages: $8.95: ISBN: 978-1-880828-81-6

AUTHENTIC SPIRITUAL MENTORING by Larry Kreider

In this book, Larry Kreider offers proven biblical keys that will open the door to thriving mentoring relationships. You will learn the Jesus Model of mentoring—initiate, build, and release— and how to apply it to the spiritual family God is preparing for you. Whether you are looking for a spiritual mentor or desiring to become one, this book is for you!

Helping You Build Cell Churches Manual
compiled by Brian Sauder and Larry Kreider

A complete biblical blueprint for small groups, this manual covers 51 topics! Includes study and discussion questions. Use for training small group leaders or personal study. 224 pages: $19.95: ISBN: 978-1-886973-38-1

Church Planting and Leadership Training
(Live or video school with Larry Kreider and others)

Prepare now for a lifetime of ministry and service to others. The purpose of this school is to train the leaders our world is desperately looking for. We provide practical information as well as Holy Spirit empowered impartation and activation. Be transformed and prepared for a lifetime of ministry and service to others.

If you know where you are called to serve...church, small group, business, public service, marketplace, or simply want to grow in your leadership ability—our goal is to help you build a biblical foundation to be led by the Holy Spirit and pursue your God-given dreams. For a complete list of classes and venues, visit www.dcfi.org.

School of Global Transformation (seven-month residential, discipleship school). Be equipped for a lifetime of service in the church, marketplace, and beyond! The School of Global Transformation is a seven month, residential, discipleship school that runs September through March. Take seven months to satisfy your hunger for more of God. Experience His love in a deeper way than you ever dreamed possible. He has a distinctive plan and purpose for your life. We are committed to helping students discover destiny in Him and prepare them to transform the world around them.

For details, visit www.dcfi.org.

SEMINARS

One Day Seminars with Larry Kreider and other DOVE Christian Fellowship International authors and leaders.

Building Your Personal House of Prayer
How to Fulfill Your Calling as a Spiritual Father/Mother
How to Build Healthy Leadership Teams
How to Hear God—30 Different Ways
Called Together Couple Mentoring
How to Build Small Groups—Basics
How to Grow Small Groups—Advanced
Counseling Basics
Effective Fivefold Ministry Made Practical
Starting House Churches
Planting Churches Made Practical
How to Live in Kingdom Prosperity
How to Equip and Release Prophetic Ministry

For more information about DCFI seminars,
Call: 800-848-5892
E-mail: seminars@dcfi.org

Additional copies of this book and other
book titles from DESTINY IMAGE are
available at your local bookstore.

Call toll-free: 1-800-722-6774.

Send a request for a catalog to:

Destiny Image® Publishers, Inc.
P.O. Box 310
Shippensburg, PA 17257-0310

*"Speaking to the Purposes of God for This
Generation and for the Generations to Come."*

**For a complete list of our titles,
visit us at www.destinyimage.com.**